A CONNOISSEUR'S GUIDE TO THE MET

A CONNOISSEUR'S GUIDE TO THE MET

THE BEST OF THE METROPOLITAN
MUSEUM IN FOUR 1-HOUR TOURS

PAUL MAGRIEL AND **JOHN T. SPIKE**

VINTAGE BOOKS A DIVISION OF RANDOM HOUSE, NEW YORK

A VINTAGE ORIGINAL

FIRST EDITION

COPYRIGHT © 1987 BY PAUL MAGRIEL AND JOHN T. SPIKE

ALL RIGHTS RESERVED UNDER INTERNATIONAL AND

PAN-AMERICAN COPYRIGHT CONVENTIONS.

PUBLISHED IN THE UNITED STATES BY RANDOM HOUSE, INC., NEW YORK

AND SIMULTANEOUSLY IN CANADA BY RANDOM HOUSE

OF CANADA LIMITED, TORONTO.

LIBRARY OF CONGRESS CATALOGING-IN-PUBLICATION DATA

MARGRIEL, PAUL DAVID, 1906–

PAUL MARGRIEL'S MET.

''A VINTAGE ORIGINAL''–T.P. VERSO.

1. METROPOLITAN MUSEUM OF ART (NEW YORK, N.Y.)—GUIDE-

BOOKS. 1. SPIKE, JOHN T. II. TITLE.

N610.M34   1987   708.147'1   86-40522

ISBN 0-394-74857-3 (PBK.)

MANUFACTURED IN THE UNITED STATES OF AMERICA

10 9 8 7 6 5 4 3 2 1

ACKNOWLEDGMENTS

First of all, I am grateful to all those kind people who came on my tours and shared ninety minutes of their time and attention. The selection of works in this guide was in this sense a collaborative effort. Nobody came more often or argued more strongly or more convincingly for her point of view than Babs Simpson. To her, my devoted thanks. Another repeat customer was Jason Epstein of Random House. Jason took the tour once, then again, then a third time. Little did I know that he was researching his idea to do this book. Jason Epstein, with Sarah Timberman and Jayne Nomura, assistant editors at Random House, have expertly guided this book through all phases of production. Patricia Lothrop lent some timely editorial assistance.

I see eye to eye on most things with John T. Spike, my friend and coauthor, hence our optimum cooperation on this book. When I point out to John that no one needs to be a musicologist to enjoy a concert and that the same applies to art history and visits to museums, he fully agrees. This is generous of him, since he went to school for years to earn his art history degrees. We divided the responsibilities for this book as follows: I selected the tours, with some advice on works from John. He compiled all the texts in this book, sometimes based on my jottings or on our conversations, always with the intention of expressing in my voice my critical, non–art historical appreciation of art. I am proud that my own impressions have been so amply filled out by John's knowledge of art, which is both deep and wide ranging, and by his sensitivity to the issues that great art cannot but raise over and over again. For his part, John would like to acknowledge his gratitude to Michele and Nicholas Spike for their love, patience, and encouragement. —PAUL MAGRIEL

CONTENTS

INTRODUCTION   13

HOW TO USE THIS BOOK   16

TOUR I   21

TOUR II   75

TOUR III   129

TOUR IV   183

This little book has grown out of many years' appreciation of the Metropolitan Museum of Art. I never was an employee of this museum, but I can claim to have been a regular customer of the place for about five decades. When I first started going to the Met, they kept the statues in wooden cases, and the information desk looked like the charge desk in a library. The halls were as quiet as a gentlemen's club, and as conducive to a good nap. It was a great place to see Greek pots and Gothic reliquaries. (This is still true, of course: the Met received a stupendous gift of medieval treasures from J. Pierpont Morgan in 1917, the rarity and value of which long ago passed the point of computation.)

Lots of things have changed about the Met, needless to say—most of all, the attendance. Millions of people climb (or stretch out on) the Fifth Avenue stairs every year. During Christmas vacation the Museum's central rotunda offers all the repose of Grand Central Station.

The Met was built to accommodate a crowd, and with roughly 3 million objects to choose from, you may rest assured of being able to find something made just for you. The problem is, where should you begin to look? *A Connoisseur's Guide to the Met* contains four brief tours designed to get you started—no matter whether you are a New Yorker who remembers his or her class trips to the Egyptian Wing or an out-of-towner who is making a first, probably hurried, visit to the city. By the time you finish all four tours and see all one hundred selections, you will have crisscrossed the entire building and sampled nearly every department.

Each painting or sculpture (or snuffbox or table) is described in no more than three paragraphs. These brief texts are meant to be read *in front of* the works of art, not by the fireplace. That is one difference between *A Connoisseur's Guide to the Met* and other guidebooks: this book is a conversation between you and me about what are (in my opinion) the one hundred best works of art out of the 3 million here. Other guidebooks attempt the impossible: the history of world art in fifty words or less. This approach simply doesn't work; hence the well-earned reputation of guidebooks for being boring. If you are excited enough to wonder about the artist or culture that created a certain work, no guidebook will be able to tell you as much as you would like to know. By the same token, the capsule art histories found in guidebooks are peculiarly designed to make you feel uncomfortable about all the things that you do not know and never will.

A Connoisseur's Guide to the Met is designed to encourage you to disagree, even though I shall work very hard to bring you around to my point of view. You can write to me in care of the publisher, if you like, but I doubt that you can change my mind. Some of the works of art I have chosen are world famous, others are downright obscure. All they have in common is that they touch my heart or mind in some way.

The challenge that I put to myself was in two parts: Which among these infinite offerings are my favorite few? And can I defend my choices as constituting the *very best* that the Met has to offer? In his *Italian Journey* (Naples, March 9, 1787), Goethe laid the groundwork for this approach better than I ever could:

If what is good gives one joy, what is better gives one even more, and, in art, only the best is good enough.

My tours evolved as I invited friends, one or two at a time, to come with me to the Met to test my judgments. As you follow the itinerary in *A Connoisseur's Guide to the Met*, feel free to imagine the air filled with my cheerful provocations, for instance: "The only thing worth looking at in this gallery is this" [pointing at No. 16, the marble bust by Rysbrack]. Or, "The Met is awash in paintings by Renoir. This one is the best" [No. 47, the portrait of Margot Bérard].

In the course of time, friends have recommended my tours to other friends, and during the last few years I have had very pleasant differences of opinion with a fascinating group of people. Most of them have not been strangers to the Met, but they have all told me afterward that they had been shown treasures they had never seen in rooms where they had never been.   —PAUL MAGRIEL

Each of the four tours in this book opens with a map, indicating the locations of the 25 objects to follow. Opposite the map you will find a listing of the 25 titles and their call numbers (such as "Saint Catherine. [50.64]"); these numbers identify the pieces. Following each map and listing are 25 entries accompanied by photographs.

The Met is the greatest art museum in the world. It contains more different kinds of art made by more people at more times in history than any other museum. In sum, the Met has too many great things for any one person to absorb in a single lifetime—I state this from personal experience. Therefore, never mind the treasures you will miss. Console yourself with the discoveries you can make. Even if you are making a once-in-a-lifetime pilgrimage to this aesthetic Mecca, I advise you to use this book and to cover as much of it as time and energy allow. The alternative is to wander about the galleries like an animal in the forest—except the animal knows what it is looking for.

I have kept this book as short as possible for two reasons: (1) the descriptions are meant to be read in front of the works; and (2) when visiting a museum you shouldn't bury your nose in a book anyway. There is definitely a limit to human concentration. After ninety minutes of thinking hard about these things, you should go home feeling satisfied (or at least stop for lunch). To finish *A Connoisseur's Guide to the Met*, therefore, you will have to come back more than once.

No tour of twenty-five exhibits should take you longer than ninety minutes—if necessary, don't walk, *run* to the next item. That's what I do: it keeps the blood pumping, and it cuts out distractions. While taking these tours, *do not stop to look around*. That's for other days. The unsolvable problem of museums is that they cannot possibly display their works with proper separation from one another. Glass cases are the worst in this way, since everyone has a natural tendency to take the contents in at a glance and then move on without having seen anything. Nobody can appreciate two books side by side or listen to Bach in one ear and Vivaldi in the other. Give your full attention (for once!) to the piece in front of you. Turn it over in your mind. Compare your response to mine, as I have written it down in this book.

The texts offer various observations on the qualities that make the work, in my opinion, distinctive—sometimes unlike any other in the world. Please do not confuse intrinsic quality with simple rarity. Art historians are infatuated with rarity—which they find highly significant. Rarity does not interest me if the work is not personally rewarding.

Vermeer made very few paintings; Rembrandt was prolific: all that interests us is to learn what each did best. My hope is that after you absorb my approach, you will be inspired to try it yourself. Art is exciting only if we allow ourselves to speak out loud our personal associations and responses. You are about to read a book of my opinions. Now just go up the stairs and see how they compare to yours.   —PAUL MAGRIEL

Note: The order of the tours is based on the installation of the Met as we go to press. By the time that you come to visit, one or another of the items may be temporarily off view. Please be patient, and look for the piece on your next visit.

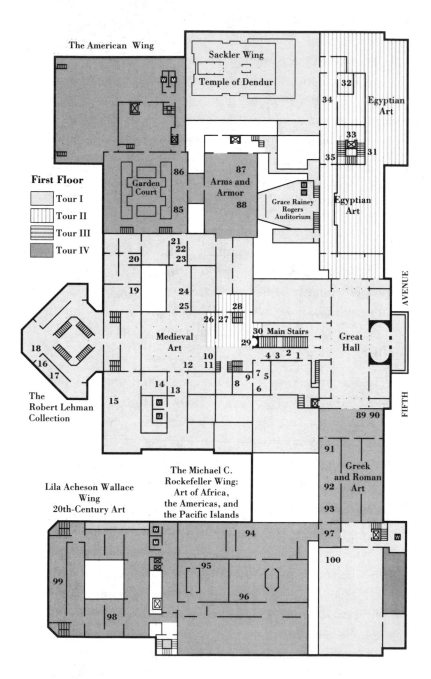

The American Wing

Sackler Wing

Temple of Dendur

32

34

Egyptian Art

33

35   31

First Floor

Tour I

Tour II

Tour III

Tour IV

86

85

Garden Court

87
Arms and Armor
88

Grace Rainey Rogers Auditorium

Egyptian Art

21
22
23

20

19

24

25

28

26 27

18

16

17

The Robert Lehman Collection

15

Medieval Art

14   13

12

10
11

30 Main Stairs

29

Great Hall

4 3 2 1

7 5
9
8   6

89 90

91

92

93

97

100

Greek and Roman Art

Lila Acheson Wallace Wing
20th-Century Art

The Michael C. Rockefeller Wing:
Art of Africa,
the Americas, and
the Pacific Islands

94

95

96

99

98

AVENUE

FIFTH

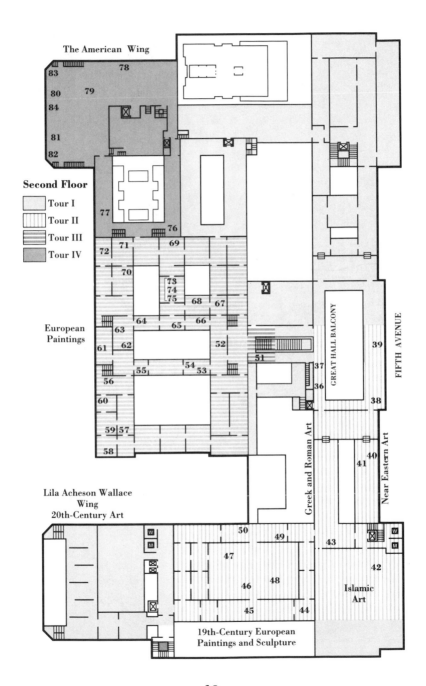

The American Wing

83
78
80   79
84
81
82

Second Floor
Tour I
Tour II
Tour III
Tour IV

77

76

72 71   69
70
73
74   68   67
75
64   65   66
63
61 62   52
54 53
55
56
60
59 57
58

European
Paintings

51

37
36

GREAT HALL BALCONY

39

38

FIFTH AVENUE

Greek and Roman Art

Near Eastern Art

40
41

Lila Acheson Wallace
Wing
20th-Century Art

50
49
47
43
46 48
45   44

42

Islamic
Art

19th-Century European
Paintings and Sculpture

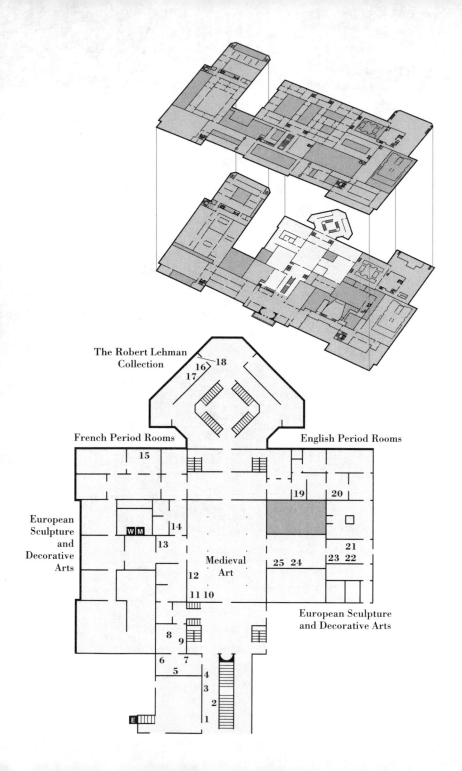

The Robert Lehman
Collection

16 18
17

French Period Rooms   English Period Rooms

15

European
Sculpture
and
Decorative
Arts

W M   14
        13

19   20

Medieval
Art

21

25 24   23 22

European Sculpture
and Decorative Arts

12

11 10

8
  9

6   7
  5
        4
        3
        2
E   1

GROUND FLOOR, CENTER

- *Entrance: Left Corridor to left of Grand Staircase —Byzantine Art*

1. Large Dish with the Battle of David and Goliath. (17.190.396).
2. Chalice. (17.190.1710).
3. Figure of a Leopard. (47.100.18).
4. Sleeve Fastener (the larger of the pair). (47.100.9).
   - *Turn left into Renaissance Sculpture*
5. Christ at the Column. (59.153).
6. Horse. Workshop of Giovanni Bologna. (24.212.23).
7. Striding Satyr. Riccio. (1982.45).
   - *Enter Linsky Collection Galleries*
8. Monk-Scribe Astride a Dragon. (1982.60.396).
9. The Marriage Feast at Cana. Juan de Flandes. (1982.60.20).
   - *Enter Large Medieval Hall*
10. A Mourning Woman. (41.100.128).
11. Saint Catherine. (50.64).
12. Virgin and Child. (17.190.725).
    - *Turn left to French Decorative Arts*
13. Breakfast Service. Sèvres. (56.29.1–8).
    - *In the Corridor leading to the Wrightsman Collection*
14. Snuff Box. Possibly by Delafons. (1976.155.22).
    - *Wrightsman Collection*
15. Writing Table. Gilles Joubert. (1973.315.1).
    - *Across to Untermyer Section*
16. Saint Anthony in the Wildnerness. Sassetta. (1975.1.27).
17. The Annunciation. Alessandro Botticelli. (1975.1.74).
18. The Creation and the Expulsion from Paradise. Giovanni di Paolo. (1975.1.31).
    - *Medieval Galleries to the north*
19. John Barnard. Michael Rysbrack. (1976.330).
20. Ceres. (1981.187).
    - *Enter Lehman Wing*
21. Saint Catherine of Alexandria. (17.190.905).
22. Corpus of Christ. (1978.521.3).
23. Virgin and Child Reliquary. (17.190.125).
24. Plaque with the Journey to Emmaus and the Noli me tangere. (17.190.47).
25. Reliquary of Saint Thomas Becket. (17.190.520).

LARGE DISH WITH THE BATTLE
OF DAVID AND GOLIATH

Silver, Byzantine (Constantinople), about 640

Gift of J. Pierpont Morgan, 1917 (17.190.396)

TOUR I
1

I ALWAYS BEGIN MY TOURS WITH
the six Byzantine plates called the Cyprus Treasure, just
to correct the notion that museums only have paintings.
At the heart of the great circle of silver at center, the ath-
letic figure of a youth stands his ground against the charge
of a warrior in full battle regalia. The youth wards off the
attack with his left arm and readies a sling in his right
hand. He is David, and his fearsome adversary is Goliath. Usually we imagine that David felled the giant Goliath through a combination of skill and luck: in this telling
of the story, he appears to have complete command of the
situation. The seventh-century emperor for whom these
plates were made can have had little sympathy for the
underdog or the long shot. Long after the fall of the
Roman Empire, the star of Classical culture continued to
burn brightly over Constantinople and the eastern shore
of the Mediterranean. Thirteen centuries ago, a Byzantine emperor who liked to compare himself to David, bib-
lical king of the Hebrews, decided to immortalize his hero
in a cycle of ten sculpted plates showing David's tri-
umphs. In chronological terms, these are medieval works
fashioned long after the demise of the pagan gods, yet
they are still infused with the time-hallowed virtues of
antiquity: the cult of human beauty, heroism, and stoic
courage. As a work of art the Cyprus Treasure is the
supernova of the Classical world, a last blinding burst
before extinction.

CHALICE

Gold, Byzantine, 7th c.

Gift of J. Pierpont Morgan, 1917

(17.190.1710)

THE FOUR FIGURES THAT DECORATE
the bowl of this chalice symbolize the principal cross-
roads of the Byzantine world: Constantinople, Rome,
Alexandria, and Cyprus (where the chalice was probably
made). These motifs have been sculpted in repoussé
(relief created from the back) with some additional
engraving. However, the workmanship is not exceptionally fine (think back to the David plate, No. 1), and it is
not for these details that I suggest we consider this object.
The sculptor of this superb cup has made his statement
with its design as a whole. The idea of the chalice shape
is simple enough, of course: a bowl supported by a stand.
The possibilities for decoration then range from un-
adorned to ornate. What I find so satisfying about the
Met's chalice is something very rare and sophisticated:
the proportions of the bowl and base are completely har-
monious. Usually these vessels seem top-heavy, because
the reservoir is naturally regarded as the more important
element. Here due attention is paid to the bowl, but the
various elements of the pedestal and base are integral to
the overall design, in which the textbook configurations of
hemisphere and cylinder have been subtly varied. Where
Euclid would call for a line, our goldsmith drew a shallow
curve: the result is an elegant and original form of near-
geometry.

FIGURE OF A LEOPARD

Bronze and silver inlay, Roman, 2nd–4th c.

Fletcher Fund, 1947 (47.100.18)

THIS AMIABLE LEOPARD IN BRONZE with silver spots was probably a fibula—the archaeologists' word for a clothes clasp. Many pieces of ancient art created before the invention of zippers and snaps were made either to hold clothing in place or to give it some sparkle. Early art had a utilitarian bias that seems not to have survived the Middle Ages. Since then the preference to enshrine artistic works in private galleries and public museums has made it harder to imagine how art once "shone in use." Just think of the panache that our leopard must have had lifting its head from a moving shoulder! This leopard is a late Roman work and would not, perhaps, rank high on any absolute artistic scale, except my idiosyncratic own. Still, I like the insouciant sprawl of this big cat, reminding me that laziness is one of the few attributes that men and animals share equally.

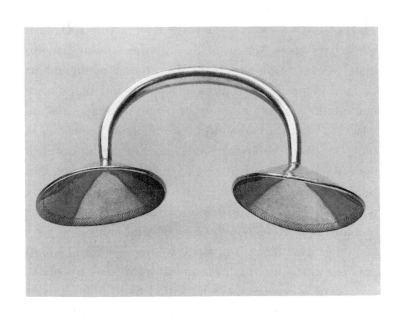

S L E E V E   F A S T E N E R

[T H E L A R G E R O F T H E P A I R]

Gold, Irish (Dublin), 8th c. B.C.

Fletcher Fund, 1947 (47.100.9)

TOUR I

4

IRELAND DURING THE BRONZE AGE (twelve centuries before the arrival of Saint Patrick) was a sophisticated place—something like a cold-water Mycenae. We do not know as much about the Celts as about their Aegean counterparts, and very few people are likely to recognize this sophisticated piece of goldsmithing as being *typically* Irish. Hundreds of these gold adornments have survived—a fraction of the number that must have been discovered only to be melted down for bullion. Most of them resemble arcs that end in circular disks. They come in all sizes, and opinions differ on whether they were meant as personal jewelry (armlets, rings, or bracelets) or as opulent clasps for clothing. Once they were all thought to represent forms of money. I cannot settle such debates, but I do know that this larger of the Met's pair has an elegance and refinement, a high style, that would be the envy of any haut couturier on the Faubourg St.-Honoré.

CHRIST AT THE COLUMN

Silver, lapis lazuli, and marble, Roman, late 17th c.

Fletcher Fund, 1959 (59.153)

From OUR CONTEMPORARY POINT OF view, this silver figurine of a suffering Christ must seem self-contradictory. We see a highly charged religious subject treated with extraordinary delicacy. The work is small—it was intended to be viewed by one person at a time. It is even possible that this sculpture was made for the pleasure of only a single person: the member of the Colonna family whose venerable coat of arms appears on the column. (*Colonna* means "column" in Italian.) The 1600s—when Galileo, Newton, Caravaggio, and Kepler lived—was arguably the beginning of modern history, but the fact remains that the visionary sensibilities of the Counter-Reformation, which arc exemplified in this statuette, are about as remote from ours today as are those of the Middle Ages, and possibly more so, for we do not expect a subject as distressing as the Flagellation to become a splendid exercise in precious metal. But we must bear in mind that neither the artist nor the patron was aware of any contradiction at all. For them this superb anatomy rendered in lustrous silver conveyed a universal truth, namely, that Christ, the divine in human form, was triumphant over all earthly travails.

HORSE

Bronze, Workshop of Giovanni Bologna (Florence), late 16th c.

Gift of Ogden Mills, 1924 (24.212.23)

The LITTLE GALLERY IN WHICH THIS
horse stands is filled with small bronzes from the 1400s
and later. An entire case is given over to bronzes cast from
models by Giovanni Bologna, the great Florentine sculptor of the late Renaissance. Why then is this horse sepa-
rated from all the others and raised on a pedestal? In a
word, because like every masterpiece of sculpture, this
creature is *alive*, while the others remain everlastingly
entrapped in base metal. The outlines of the horse's back
are cut so crisply that you can hear them crackle. The
powerful muscles tremble nervously. The patina (the surface coloring and polishing) seems as deep and reflective
as a glacial lake. Imagine how well endowed with technical expertise the 1500s must have been, if art historians
are correct to assign this horse to Giovanni Bologna's
"workshop"—considering it the work of a close assistant,
probably not even cast under the master's direct supervi-
sion. I wonder if this means that on the day this bronze
was cast, Giovanni Bologna merely paused long enough
at the door to say, "Boys, I'm going out. Carry on!"

STRIDING SATYR

Bronze, by Andrea Briosco, called Riccio, about 1507

Rogers, Pfeiffer, Harris Brisbane Dick and

Fletcher Funds, 1982 (1982.45)

H ALF-MAN, HALF-BEAST, THE SATYR personifies the unconstrained id of the Renaissance. Riccio's statuette of a satyr exudes an impassioned, wanton physicality. The sculptor confronts us with a paradox. Bronze is a base alloy, yet Riccio has transformed his material into something precious. Lovingly chased, then rubbed to an inimitable gloss, Riccio's satyr represents the ennoblement of the erotic. Usually we have to appreciate Renaissance bronzes without the benefit of attributions, because most examples issued from anonymous workshops. Riccio, who worked in Padua during the High Renaissance, is an exception: his character is sharply and unmistakably impressed on all his works. Riccio cast several statuettes of satyrs. The commanding size and luxurious finish of the Met's make it the masterpiece of the group.

MONK-SCRIBE

ASTRIDE A DRAGON

Brass, Rhenish, about 1150–1175

Jack and Belle Linsky Collection, 1982 (1982.60.396)

THE SEQUENCES OF THESE TOURS ARE
mostly dictated by the layout of the Met, but within these
limits I have made every effort to vary the pace, to seize
contrasts and embrace opposites—in brief, to keep your
eye fresh. The problem with most visits to a museum (and
inevitably to a poorly planned exhibition) is that an
excess of pots or rugs, Sargents or Homers soon becomes
indigestible. This monk-scribe and his airborne dragon
appear on our itinerary between a statuette by Riccio and
a panel by Juan de Flandes, both superlative examples of
technical finesse. In comparison, this greenish brass
from the Middle Ages offers the tactile sensuosity of a
rusty bucket. But it yields nothing in conviction or
expressive content. Perhaps it was once part of a lectern
or some other appurtenance to the reading of the Gospel. I
like to think of this earnest, hunching scrivener as the
guardian angel of every struggling writer. How energeti-
cally, confidently, and commandingly he sits astride the
demon, inspiration. This is one author who has tamed his
muse: both its dragonlike recalcitrance and its wild
flights of fancy.

THE MARRIAGE
FEAST AT CANA

Oil on wood, by Juan de Flandes, about 1500

Jack and Belle Linsky Collection, 1982 (1982 .60 .20)

9

MOST PAINTERS HAVE AGREED that the Wedding at Cana was a rollicking good time. This panel, so still and serious, begs to differ. How strange that a wedding feast should be so thinly attended. This is an image of solemnity, not a party that has drunk up all the wine. X rays of this panel have revealed that the painter progressively deleted secondary figures and props from his composition until he had attained the extraordinary compression of the picture as it now stands. Instead of a party in full swing, Juan de Flandes, a rare but admired master of Renaissance Spain, concentrated his powers on the sacramental overtones of Christ's miraculous transformation of water into wine. There remains, however, a solitary figure whose part in this event is unclear: outside the loggia lurks a man with a bemused expression, perhaps the artist himself.

A MOURNING WOMAN

Painted walnut, Flemish, 15th c.

Gift of George Blumenthal, 1941 (41.100.128)

I SEE THIS SOLITARY LADY IN MOURNING
as the embodiment of Grief. Her profound isolation is the
result of the accidents of time, however, not creative
intention. She must have been carved as a supporting
actor in a sculptural group of the Crucifixion or the Lam-
entation. Now she weeps for her lost companions, like
Rachel for her children. It was a Gothic characteristic,
even as the Renaissance was drawing near, to represent a
religious subject in contemporary courtly dress. Medieval costumes inevitably strike us as fancy or quaint. But
our lady's fairy-tale gown only heightens the poignancy of
her tightly clasped hands, a natural and timeless gesture
of grief. Her slender waist makes her human frame seem
too fragile for such woe, yet her sweet face is not distorted
by pain. On the contrary, she looks ennobled by her
ordeal.

SAINT CATHERINE

Walnut, Flemish, 16th c.

Gift of Miss Edith Sachs, 1950 (50.64)

THIS STYLISH YOUNG WOMAN LOOKS more saucy than saintly. She was obviously conceived by an artist who felt no compunction about making a religious subject engaging and or bridging the distance between high faith and high fashion. This Saint Catherine wears an extravagant gown that shows off her slim waist and high bosom. Her satisfied smile and the jester at her feet are reminders as well that she was born into a secular court before she transferred her allegiance to Heaven. But next to the jester is the broken Catherine wheel, symbol of her martyrdom, and such is the inherent grace of this figure that we can hardly doubt that she has been reading her missal and not a romance. Her playfulness is merely evidence of a religiosity that has so permeated her life that it can take all worldly show in stride.

VIRGIN AND CHILD

Painted oak, French (probably Paris), late 13th c.

Gift of J. Pierpont Morgan, 1917 (17.190.725)

As an image of love, this engaging Virgin and her playful Child could hardly be surpassed. They are a celebration of tender joy. The mother holds her tiny Child so lightly, yet the circle of their arms and the meeting of their eyes signal their complete absorption in each other. The Child tilts his head to look into Mary's face. The short, tight smiles that make most Gothic faces seem distant and vague have here miraculously achieved an ineffable sweetness. The simple human warmth of this little statue speaks the most strongly to us. But to the sculptor and his audience it would have been an affecting reminder of the unique relationship that made Mary the most effective intercessor, and an image of the possibility of union between the human and the divine.

BREAKFAST SERVICE

Porcelain, Sèvres (France), 1813

Gift of Mr. and Mrs. D. N. Heineman, 1956 (56.29.1–8)

THIS PORCELAIN AND GILT SERVICE
answers the question, How might an emperor take his
café and croissant of a morning? Only a cup and plate so
unequivocally *expensive* as these would do. This service
is a gilt-edged invitation from the artisans at Sèvres to
immerse ourselves in ostentation. From the historical
standpoint these porcelains exemplify with textbook clarity two currents of central importance to French aesthetics: technical perfection and grandiose design. In 1813
the factory at Sèvres had been operating for less than a
century, but it had long been recognized as the source ne
plus ultra for porcelain services and plaques (Meissen
held the sway for figurines). This service aspires to com-
pete with painting on its own terms: Each piece is
adorned with a "window" that looks onto an Arcadian
landscape peopled by nymphs and cupids. The Classical
myths were the conceptual underpinnings of the Napole-
onic imagination, so our pampered breakfaster must have
felt doubly replenished every morning.

SNUFF BOX

Gold and vellum, possibly by Delafons, miniatures by

Louis Nicolas van Blarenberghe, French (Paris), 18th c.

Gift of Mr. and Mrs. Charles Wrightsman, 1976 (1976.155.22)

FRENCH SNUFF BOXES WERE THE FABERGÉ eggs of the eighteenth century: their owners considered the *how* of these confections rather more significant than the *why*. The Met has a superb selection of these boxes: I recommend this one because it is always a pleasant surprise to look into an array of jewels and suddenly come upon a *vista*. The eighteenth century was in love with fantasy, and this snuff box artfully combines two apparently divergent tastes of the period, for the grand and for the miniature. The duc de Choiseul, principal minister of Louis XV until he fell out of royal favor in 1770, lavished on his Château de Chanteloup the sort of attentions and blandishments that were usually reserved for favorite mistresses. The grounds encompassed a forest in addition to gardens in the formal French and the more natural "Anglochinois" style. The marvelous incongruity of inserting a bird's-eye view of these vast estates into a bit of goldsmith's work must have delighted the duke. He later had a second box made, this one decorated with interior views of the Hôtel de Choiseul in Paris. I would like to think that he carried the city box in the country, and vice versa, thus enjoying both of his sumptuous residences at all times.

WRITING TABLE

Oak, lacquered with scarlet and gold vernis martin,

gilt bronze, by Gilles Joubert, 18th c.

Gift of Mr. and Mrs. Charles Wrightsman, 1973 (1973.315.1)

IN THE 1750S INTERIOR DECORATION WAS a suitable pastime for a king: Louis XV of France was personally involved in the design of this writing table for his private study. Nowadays a few eyebrows would rise if our President called the factory to give his ideas on office décor. But Louis XV took an exceptional interest in the arts. His father, Louis XIV, had sought glory by dominating Europe, and expanding his palace at Versailles. By contrast, Louis XV set about carving interior retreats for himself within the immensity of Versailles. This table was made for his study. Surprisingly enough, its decoration is imposing without being ostentatious. The outline is relatively simple, and the bold curve of the knees has none of the frothiness that might be expected from the epicenter of Rococo decoration. The three drawers do not, of course, offer much storage, but this would not have inconvenienced a man who gave his orders by divine right and had a cast of thousands to follow them through.

SAINT ANTHONY IN
THE WILDERNESS

Tempera on panel, by Sassetta, about 1444

Robert Lehman Collection, 1975 (1975.1.27)

THIS PERFECT LITTLE PICTURE MAKES
me smile, which, alas, is an admission of an aspect in
which our age is impoverished compared with the past.
This devotional work of the early Renaissance retains a
medieval commitment to symbolic language hardly recognizable to us today. Sassetta has shown the good Saint
Anthony Abbot appalled by his unwonted confrontation
with a rabbit (representative of time-honored sexual pro-
clivities). How naive this is, we say. After all, how tempt-
ing could a rabbit be? But for Sassetta, this rabbit was as
potent a symbol of lasciviousness as the elderly saint was
of sanctity. Sassetta made this picture to be nothing less
than a face-off between righteousness and the way of all
flesh. Several generations after the coming of mass com-
munications, it is hard for us to recapture the drama
invested in a simple scene of two unlikely cham-
pions at odds in a barren landscape—but the effort is
more than worthwhile.

THE ANNUNCIATION

Tempera on panel, by Alessandro Botticelli, about 1500

Robert Lehman Collection, 1975 (1975.1.74)

THIS BOTTICELLI IS THE SECOND OF three pictures that I have selected from a single room in the Lehman Collection. Although Botticelli represented a mystical strain in Florentine painting, this *Annunciation* is the quintessence of geometric rationality compared with the visionary paintings by the two Sienese, Sassetta (No. 18) and Giovanni di Paolo (No. 20), on this tour. The proud painters of Siena resisted as long as they could the perspectival tricks invented by the Florentines. The apogee of the new rational, geometric point of view is nobly demonstrated in Botticelli's *Annunciation*: the two solidly physical actors in this divine drama are very nearly upstaged by the architecture of their theater. This is a crystalline view of Heaven as Descartes might have envisioned it a century later. The Virgin and the archangel bow at virtually the same angle, two halves of a living crescent. They are modeled as firmly as little sculptures; indeed, this panel has the supernatural clarity and brilliance of a diorama peopled with figurines.

THE CREATION AND THE
EXPULSION OF ADAM AND
EVE FROM PARADISE

Tempera on panel, by Giovanni di Paolo, about 1445

Robert Lehman Collection, 1975 (1975.1.31)

OUR PRESENT AGE, TRAINED IN CUBISM, thinks that this cosmographic painting by a bona fide Old Master is irresistible, and I am no exception. Although by the mid–fifteenth century Siena had yielded the palm to Florence, its relentlessly progressive rival in the arts, see how Giovanni di Paolo unashamedly held out for the *retardataire*. This Gothic panel with its enameled Paradise and cosmic color wheel (*pace* Robert Delaunay) is a compendium of traditional iconography: the view from Heaven of a dinner-plate Earth, cracked and barren after the Fall, the zodiacal universe, and other symbolic flora and fauna hark back to a medieval worldview. Giovanni's figures are always an endearing mix of limitation and compensation: his wiry manikins are ill proportioned but enlivened by a restless vitality. Their faces are stereotyped, yet they manage to eke out a measure of individuality. Still, the abiding greatness of this *Expulsion from Paradise* lies in the compelling sense of movement with which Giovanni has informed this theme of involuntary removal.

JOHN BARNARD

Marble, Michael Rysbrack, 1744

Purchase, Gift of J. Pierpont Morgan, The Moses Lazarus

Collection, Gift of the Misses Sarah and Josephine Lazarus,

Bequest of Kate Read Blacque, in memory of her husband,

Valentine Alexander Blacque, Bequest of Mary Clark Thompson,

and Bequest of Barbara S. Adler, by exchange, 1976 (1976.330)

TOUR I

19

ONE OF THE GREATEST ENGLISH
sculptors, Rysbrack infused life into this cold stone. If we
think of memorials as dusty statues in churches (church
statues, as it happens, were a specialty of Rysbrack's,
including his famous *Isaac Newton* in Westminster
Abbey), it is a surprise to see this tender portrayal of a
child who died before he could fulfill his promise. Know-
ing the fate of John Barnard, we read tragedy into the
unexpected maturity of his ten-year-old face, his distant
gaze and serious expression. Rysbrack has conveyed the
self-possession and intelligence of this child, and even a
certain resignation, which seems to anticipate death but
does nothing to mitigate the loss. This small work is a
showpiece for the virtuosity of the sculptor. Rysbrack had
inherited the long Flemish tradition of technical mastery:
with seeming ease he evoked an astonishing variety of
textures and even the hint of color in the way the surfaces
break the fall of light across the pale marble. A great
memorial, like this one, spurns the grave as it affirms the
possibilities of life.

CERES

Soft-paste porcelain, Chelsea (London), about 1749–1750

Gift of Irwin Untermyer by exchange, 1981 (1981.187)

M OST EIGHTEENTH-CENTURY porcelains, I think, are frivolous, but that's a distinctly minority opinion. These objects—Meissen, Sèvres, Chelsea—have never gone out of favor with collectors. Historically, princes, peers, and founding partners have always competed for the choicest items from the instant they emerged from the kiln. My objection is not to the Rococo aesthetic of sweetness and light per se; in fact this Chelsea statuette of Ceres appeals to me very much. It has an ease and refinement that is on a higher plane than the merely decorative. Undoubtedly the pure whiteness (most Chelsea is highly colored) enhances the sculptural aspirations of this little piece. Many of the designs of this English factory were borrowed from France, and this *Ceres* is no exception: the delicate features of the pretty goddess call to mind the works of the sculptor J.-B. Pigalle. Ceres was the Roman goddess of agriculture and grain, and the prototype for this figurine might have been a piece of garden statuary. If so, it has been brilliantly translated into a small but graceful presence for any tabletop.

SAINT CATHERINE
OF ALEXANDRIA

Metalwork-Goldsmith's Work, French (Burgundy), early 15th c.

Gift of J. Pierpont Morgan, 1917 (17.190.905)

TOUR 1

21

T HIS IS A FULL-FLEDGED SMALL SCULP-
ture. Gaudily adorned, this exquisite princess challenges
us to see her with the eyes of the Middle Ages. Although
her tiny figure seems overburdened with the weight of
pearls and other gems, such incrustation was only a sign
of the reverence due her as a precious soul. Saint
Catherine bravely suffered martyrdom in the third century. Her symbol is a broken wheel, a torture from which
she was rescued by angels. A thousand years later her
cult flourished, and she became one of the most popular
medieval intercessors. We have to look past the gold and
jewels today to see the elegant workmanship of her nose
and chin, the milky delicacy of her enameled complexion, and the serenity of her eternal devotion.

CORPUS OF CHRIST

Ivory with traces of polychrome,

French (probably Paris), about 1230–1250

Gift of Mr. and Mrs. Maxime L. Hermanos, 1978 (1978.521.3)

THIS IVORY FIGURINE IS ALL THAT
remains of a medieval crucifix. Its scale is large considering the preciousness of the medium but, typical of Gothic
art, this *Corpus Christi* reserves its message for those who
come near and pause to contemplate. The depredations of
seven hundred years have only confirmed the inviolable
dignity of the sculptor's conception. The style is transi-
tional: Romanesque abstract tendencies have been
touchingly modified here and there by naturalistic observations far in advance of the Renaissance. For example,
the broad, simple planes of the chest effectively contrast
with the lively surfaces of the hair and linen. The sche-
matic rendering of the torso does not prepare us for the
humanity of the slightly protruding belly. Christ's features are not exaggerated or contorted; his agony is subtly
compressed into his half-closed eyes and barely parted
lips. In thirteenth-century Paris the demand for devotional objects gave rise to a network of workshops, but
very few of their sculptures have come down to us: this
noble *Corpus Christi*, although only a fragment, is a compelling index of the loss to posterity.

VIRGIN AND
CHILD RELIQUARY

Copper gilt with enamel, Spanish, 12th c.

Gift of J. Pierpont Morgan, 1917 (17.190.125)

Fourteen inches high, this spanish copper-gilt sculpture of the Virgin and Child is, in medieval terms, monumentally large—I suggest that you approach it with some circumspection. The doll-like face of the Virgin, and the old man's face of her Infant, tell us right away that this statuette was not meant to reflect everyday realities. Nor is the rationality of Renaissance humanism anywhere on the horizon. These are two divinities whose gravity, formality, and concentration leave no room for worldly preoccupations with elegance or refinement. The demanded response is unadulterated awe. The Spanish Romanesque lacked the cosmopolitanism of the French, but the same Spanish instinct for mysticism would, five hundred years later, inspire preternatural paintings from the brush of a nonnative painter called El Greco.

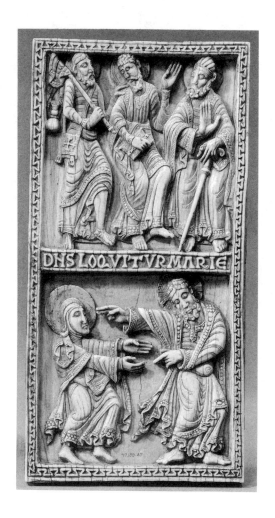

PLAQUE WITH THE JOURNEY TO EMMAUS AND THE NOLI ME TANGERE

Ivory, North Spanish (possibly León), late 11th c.

Gift of J. Pierpont Morgan, 1917 (17.190.47)

THESE SMALL, VITAL FIGURES, SWATHED in agitated robes, seem anxious to escape their compartments. Their Romanesque creator was not striving for realism: he gladly sacrificed the familiarity of nature in his attempt to portray the spirit, the *super*natural. The animated gestures of the larger-than-life hands are especially charged with meaning. In the upper frame Christ and the two apostles are linked by the zigzag lines of their raised hands and syncopated feet (the latter signaling the movements of walking). In the lower frame the hands of Christ and Mary Magdalene seem to send spiritual energy back and forth like electrical conductors. Their hands occupy center stage, which is perfectly appropriate for the story of the resurrected Christ's admonition, "Touch me not."

RELIQUARY OF
SAINT THOMAS BECKET

Silver, parcel-gilt, niello, English, 1173–1180

Gift of J. Pierpont Morgan, 1917 (17.190.520)

I T IS A MIRACLE THAT THIS SMALL, fragile, and precious box has survived intact. It was worked by anonymous artisans in medieval England, yet material and aesthetic values are only part of its story. This casket represents a world of religious significance that was once universal but is now mostly lost. The ruby on the lid symbolizes its original purpose: to hold some drops of Thomas Becket's blood. Becket was martyred when he upheld the rights of the Church against the regal prerogatives of his king, Henry II. Three years later he was canonized in recognition of his sacrifice. In time Becket came to be seen as a defender of individual conscience against the crushing weight of governmental authority, and thus to represent a theme that would continue to reverberate in English history. On the lid and sides of this casket, Heaven (the incised angels, one bearing the child image of the martyr's soul) and Earth (the scenes of his death and burial) are joined in testimony to the importance of a relic—and of an idea.

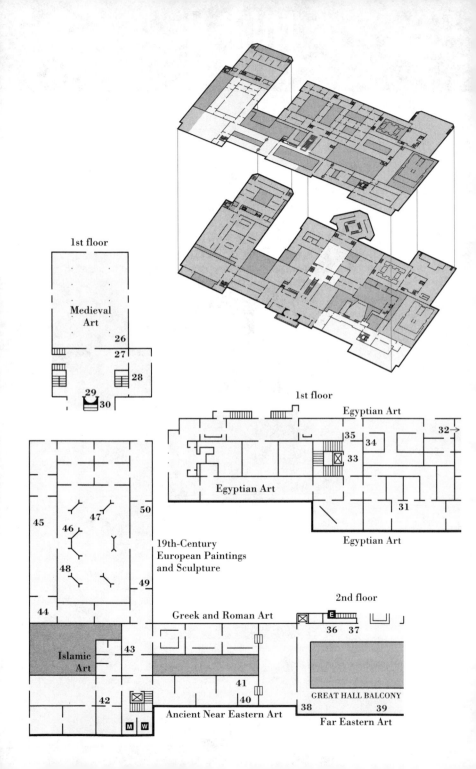

1st floor

Medieval
Art

26
27
28
29
30

1st floor

Egyptian Art

35
34
33
32→
31

Egyptian Art

Egyptian Art

19th-Century
European Paintings
and Sculpture

45
46
47
48
49
50
44

Islamic
Art

43
42

M   W

Greek and Roman Art

2nd floor

36   37

GREAT HALL BALCONY

38   39

Ancient Near Eastern Art

Far Eastern Art

41
40

GROUND FLOOR, CENTER, EGYPTIAN WING, ANDRÉ MEYER GALLERIES

26. Large Dish with Rider. (46.85.1).
27. Knight aquamanile. (64.101.1492).
28. Apollo. Adrian de Vries. (41.190.534).
29. Head of a King. (44.85.1).
   • *Corridor, Right (North) side of staircase*
30. Dish. (66.11.25).
   • *Egyptian Wing*
31. The Steward Senbi. (11.150.27).
32. Fragmentary Head of a Queen. (26.7.1396).
   (Go up staircase to second floor to see the following sculpture, then descend and return to Egyptian Wing.)
33. Seated Buddha. (19.186).
34. A Nubian Woman. (30.8.93).
35. General Tjahapimu. (08.205.1).
   • *Up escalator to Second-floor balcony, Asian Art*
36. Yashoda and Krishna. (1982.220).
37. Standing Maitreya. (1982.220.12).
38. Perseus Holding the Head of Medusa. Antonio Canova. (67.110).
39. Tomb Figure. (20.39.1).
   • *Near Eastern Art*
40. Statuette of Man. (55.142).
41. Seated Gudea. (59.2).
   • *Islamic Galleries*
42. Bowl. (65.106.2).
   • *Greek Pots*
43. Panathenaic Prize Amphora. (14.130.12).
   • *André Meyer Galleries*
44. Study in the Nude for the Dressed Ballet Dancer. After a model by Edgar Degas. (29.100.373).
45. Nijinsky. Auguste Rodin. (L.1979.76).
46. Invitation to the Side-show (La Parade). Georges Seurat. (61.101.17).
47. Margot Bérard. Auguste Renoir. (61.101.15).
48. The Englishman at the Moulin Rouge. Henri de Toulouse-Lautrec. (67.187.108).
49. Pepito Costa y Bonells. Francisco Goya. (61.25).
50. The Whale Ship. J. M. W. Turner. (96.29).

LARGE DISH WITH RIDER

Maiolica, Tuscan, early 15th c.

Fletcher Fund, 1946 (46.85.1)

ITALY IS MORE THAN A COLLECTION
of masterpieces, it is a way of life that has hardly changed
in five hundred years. Unusually large, and from an
unusually early date, this fifteenth-century dish cele-
brates the honesty and vigor of folk art and the continuity
of art made for use. It brings back memories of a convivial
trattoria and earthenware bowls brimming with home-
made *gnocchi.* The ornamental pattern along the edge is
laid on with the carefree touch of a Renaissance Matisse.
Why be a slave to consistency? As unpretentious as the
drawing is, the rider carries himself with dignity, and his
horse is proud and ebullient. Maiolica is a difficult process because the color sinks into the terra-cotta, permit-
ting no revisions or corrections. Later generations of
maiolica painters challenged themselves to do the impossible: they copied fine art designs from prints by the masters (such as Raphael and Dürer mostly). The results are
often dazzling but less and less like anything to serve at a
table. In pursuit of perfection, craftsmen forfeited the
spontaneity and unassuming humor of the early works,
like this great dish.

KNIGHT AQUAMANILE

Bronze, German (Saxony), late 13th c.

Bequest of Irwin Untermyer, 1964 (64.101.1492)

This SAXON KNIGHT COMBINES TRUTH-ful observation with ornamental grace. He sits straight up in the saddle, projecting authority and conviction. Even with his visor down, I can see his noble mien. And how perfectly his proud horse complements him, with bulging muscles arrested by the rigid thrust of planted hooves. In Medieval times, aquamaniles, water vessels, were used as ceremonial objects by celebrants to wash their hands during the Mass. They may also have been used in wealthy households. These objects were usually cast in the forms of animals—lions were especially favored—and they constitute one of the principal sculptural expressions of the Middle Ages. Medieval art is often considered esoteric, because during the centuries that elapsed between the Romans and the Renaissance, people preferred art that they could hold in their hands and put to use. I doubt, though, that this conception is appreciably more strange than the consensus nowadays that objects encountered in daily life need have no aesthetic qualities at all.

APOLLO

Bronze, by Adrian de Vries, 17th c.

Bequest of George Blumenthal, 1941 (41.190.534)

THIS STATUETTE IS AN OBVIOUS SHOW-
piece, a demonstration of the sculptor's ingeniousness,
command of anatomy, and surpassing technique (the
flawless casting and patination of the bronze). This *Apollo*
may seem excessively artificial for our taste, but it was
made in an intellectual climate that rewarded artists for
this very quality. Throughout the Renaissance painters
and sculptors took pleasure in arguing the primacy of
their respective arts. Painting had to resort to mirrors and
reflections in limpid pools to rival the natural capacity of
sculpture to show figures from both the front and the
back. Associated with this sixteenth-century debate was
the *figura serpentinata*, a pose like a twisted rope, used
by both painters and sculptors but, it has to be said, to
greater advantage by sculptors. As in de Vries's *Apollo*,
there is no principal view—the outline is constantly animated and broken. The peculiar result is that both the
front and the back can be seen at the same time. Adrian
de Vries, a Dutchman who studied in Florence under
Giambologna, was principally active in the powerful, if
esoteric, court of Rudolph II in Prague, and like his master he was esteemed for his technical prowess. The sensuous, creamy surfaces of his bronzes are among his most
distinctive achievements: if his creations often seem
emotionally hollow, they are unsurpassable in their evocation of firm, strong bodies that are inviting to the touch.

HEAD OF A KING

Limestone, West French (Nôtre-Dame de la Couldre, Parthenay), 12th c.

Gift of Mr. and Mrs. Frederick B. Platt, 1935 (44.85.1)

GREAT STONE SCULPTURES HAVE AN inner life that cannot be extinguished by fragmentation or abuse. This Old Testament king (or, some think, Christian emperor Constantine) once belonged to a collection of statues decorating the facade of a Romanesque church. Even deprived of the royal retinue and panoply, an aura of power crowns the monumental head. He has the implacability of a bearded Zeus, but, appropriate to his Christian context, huge, pupilless eyes seem to gaze fixedly, imperturbably, on a realm beyond this Earth.

D I S H

(back view)

Silver, Greek, 6th c. B.C.

Purchase, Mrs. Vincent Astor Gift, 1966 (66.11.25)

THE STORY IS TOLD THAT GIOTTO, when asked to demonstrate his artistic genius, drew (without lifting his pencil) a perfect circle. The utter simplicity of this Greek dish makes the same point. As you look at this immaculate circle of silver, make no mistake about it: the ancient Greeks did not design a plain dish because they were opposed to adornment. Instead, they were convinced that harmony lies at the heart of beauty. This is elegance in the same sense that physicists consider certain equations elegant. At many times in history the reductive aesthetic of this dish would not have been appreciated. Can you imagine a greater contrast to the rough-hewn chunk of limestone that you have just seen? From time to time, a Mies van der Rohe formulates an artistic credo based on simplicity, but not every Minimalist would grasp the secret behind this silver dish. Faultless proportion, like perfect pitch, is an innate gift that can be neither learned from books nor copied from the Greeks.

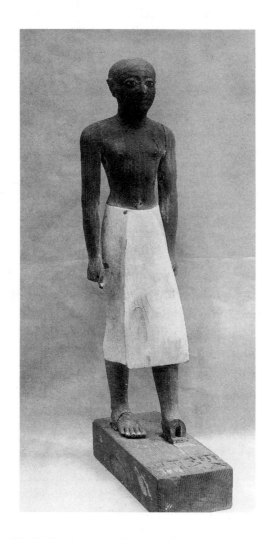

THE STEWARD SENBI

Wood, Egyptian, 12th Dynasty (about 1991–1786 B.C.)

Rogers Fund, 1911 (11.150.27)

FOUR THOUSAND YEARS AGO A MAN named Senbi entrusted the preservation of his soul to this portrait carving of himself. The Egyptians provided artistic surrogates for our all-too-perishable flesh, and they succeeded in this extraordinary ambition to an extent that only the Greeks rivaled and cannot claim to have surpassed. Senbi was a steward, a man entrusted with responsibilities. He has the appearance of a righteous man. His gaze is direct and open, and he stands firmly on his two feet. A human personality emanates from this statue of undisguised wood, one-third life size. The eyes are deep; they were made to be the windows of Senbi's soul. The sculptor considered the arms and chest important too. He had to make them supple and strong so that Senbi could execute his duties undeterred by death.

FRAGMENTARY HEAD

OF A QUEEN

Yellow jasper, Egyptian, Dynasty 18 (about 1417–1379 B.C.*)*

Purchase, Edward S. Harkness Gift, 1926 (26.7.1396)

90

THERE IS NOTHING LEFT OF THIS PIECE of sculptured jasper except for half, not even, of the face. But nobody who sees these lips can ever forget them. The guidebooks speculate as to which queen or consort this carving once represented—nobody doubts that we are face to face with a woman who was exquisitely beautiful. It is usually impossible to think about Egyptian art apart from the religion of those ancient people. Time and neglect have cut this precious jasper loose from its historical moorings, but an unwavering sense of serenity and sensuosity remains intact. The delicate coloring and the flawless line that traces the borders of this turned-down mouth always remind me of Oriental sculpture. But the meaning of this work now lies on a universal plane. It surprises me each and every time to see the boldness—the supreme assurance!—of the swelling lower lip. Look at this mouth in profile; it crests like an arching, breaking wave.

SEATED BUDDHA

Dry lacquer, Chinese (from Hopei Province),

T'ang Dynasty (7th c. or earlier)

Rogers Fund, 1919 (19.186)

AN AURA OF STILLNESS SURROUNDS
this Buddha, seated high in a bustling passageway. The
Buddha image has been a constant in Far Eastern art and
culture for more than a millennium. Unlike the other
statues in this gallery, this early, incomparably majestic
Buddha does not reach out for our attention: this Buddha
wants to be regarded with the inner eye of our minds. His
head leans slightly forward, his torso is upright and alert.
The simple, smooth planes of his figure soothe us. Contemplative and serene, his compassionate face reassures
us of his essential humanity. The contrast between the
sharply defined features of the face and the broad volumes of the body was achieved through an unusual technique. Layers of lacquered cloths were molded over a
wooded armature and then chiseled and painted when
dry. The durable sculptures made in this way have a
weighty appearance but are light enough to be carried in
processions. This technique was dictated by practical
necessity, but the depth of conviction in the sculptor's
hand made prosaic expediency a vehicle for the holy.

A NUBIAN WOMAN

Silver, Egyptian (Nubia), Säite or Ptolemaic Period

(about 600 or 300 B.C.)

Bequest of Theodore M. Davis, 1915.

Theodore M. Davis Collection (30.8.93)

TOUR II

34

THIS SHIMMERING STATUETTE STANDS
up as straight and thin as a pencil. As detailed as she is,
with superbly sensitive modeling, she sometimes seems
almost unreal—like one of those optical projections
called holograms. I always have the disquieting sensation
that as I look closer and closer into her face, the features
only become more precisely defined and elaborated. I
wonder whether the sculptor used a magnifying lens for
this work, or whether he was content to conclude his
career with this incredible object and go blind. This silver sculpture was made at a comparatively late date in
Egyptian history. As in the monumental General Tja-
harmu that follows, Egyptian gravity and formality have
here been perceptibly softened by outside influences,
particularly Greek.

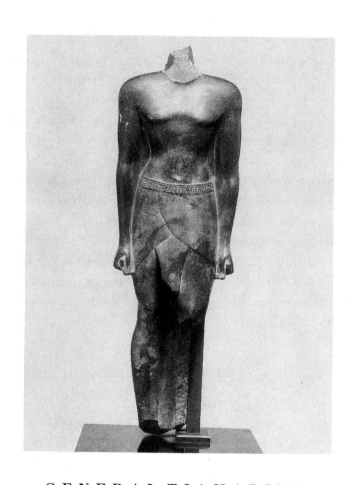

GENERAL TJAHAPIMU

Diabase, Egyptian (Memphis), Dynasty 30 (380–342 B.C.)

Gift of the British School of Archaeology, 1908 (08.205.1)

GENERAL TJAHAPIMU WAS A MILITARY man who served his nation, Egypt, during its final decline. His portrait sculpture testifies to his pride and courage. His chest is resilient and strong; he holds his arms tensed and ready at his sides. The profile view shows his resolute stride. Yet the waning of Egyptian culture is perceivable even in this memorial to a patriot. By this late date the incoming tides of Greek artistic influence had proven irresistible, and even General Tjahapimu's proud statue is a hybrid of styles. True, his frontal stance and the fact that the legs are not carved in the round are holdovers from Egyptian traditions that dated back 3,000 years. But the unbending geometry of the earlier style has given way to the swell of muscle and the softness of tissue. It is as though an Egyptian-carved chest suddenly took a deep breath. The sculptor's choice of diabase, a stone of impenetrable hardness, still reflects native priorities: the Egyptians made sculptures to be the eternal repositories of their souls. The black diabase also fittingly evokes the indomitable strength of a soldier who, I imagine, served faithfully a cause that was soon to be lost. Only a few decades later, in 332 B.C., Alexander the Great entered Egypt and took command.

Y A S H O D A   A N D   K R I S H N A

Copper, height 13¹/₈″ (33.3 cm) Indian, Karnataka state

Vijayanagar period, ca. 14th c.

Purchase, Lita Annenberg Hazan Charitable Trust Gift,

in honor of Cyntha Hazan and Leon Bernard Polsky, 1982.220.8

MOTHER AND CHILD: ACCUSTOMED AS WE
are to Italian art, we half expect the label in the display
case to read *Madonna and Child*. This Indian mother and
child are likewise divinities—the infant god Krishna was
rescued and nurtured by a foster mother, Yashoda. But we
would be wrong to press the analogy too far. Indian art has
an unmistakably uninhibited sensuousness that has
never yet been found in a Madonna and Child. Any
mother (or father) should recognize the expression of
dreamy satisfaction on the face of the nursing Krishna.
This is a family portrait of such informality that we have to
look twice for the evidence that this pair is indeed divine.
The abstracted, straightahead gaze of the mother gives a
clue to the deeper significance of this scene. Her posture
is another indication of the same thing: Indian divinities
often found repose in sitting with one leg bent sharply and
the other leg pendant; the same would be true for very few
mothers of our daily acquaintance.

STANDING MAITREYA

Gilt copper with polychrome, Nepalese, 9th–10th c.

Rogers Fund, 1982 (1982.220.12)

Maitreya IS ONE OF THE BODHISATTVA
divinities who perform crucial roles as intercessors for
Buddhists: having attained the means to Enlightenment,
the bodhisattva renounces Buddhahood until he has ful-
filled his vow to help other suffering beings reach the
same goal. Suspended, then, between the conflicting
realms of human and divine existence, this Maitreya in
gilt copper seems to embody concepts from both. His
handsome face shines with serenity. His sinuous body is a
yellow flame in ceaseless motion; the head, shoulders,
and hip trace a spiral slowly revolving in space. This
human form is unmistakably the vessel of an all-perva-
sive spirit. At the same time, it remains human: sensuous, supple, inviting to the touch. His garments do
nothing to disguise the suggestive outline of his limbs—
on the contrary, among his few adornments is a sacred
thread that runs the longest possible route down the surface of his body, doubling up on the thigh for emphasis. It
is as if Maitreya urges humankind onto the true path
through earthly persuasions.

PERSEUS HOLDING
THE HEAD OF MEDUSA

Marble, by Antonio Canova, 1804–1808

Fletcher Fund, 1967 (67.110)

This ITEM ON OUR TOUR IS A VIEW, not an object. As you walk past the display cases of Far Eastern art on your way to the Chinese terra-cottas (No. 39), stop a moment to look across the Met's rotunda to Canova's statue of *Perseus*, posed center stage on the grand balcony. Clever Perseus tricked the Gorgon by looking at her in the mirror surface of his shield. But Canova's *Perseus* is so chilly that even Medusa couldn't have frozen him more solidly. Possibly because it was commissioned as a repetition, this is public art at its most frigid. But give the Met credit—the *Perseus* is brilliantly sited, and, after all, something less than a Donatello can still enhance a piazza. Canova's sleek, effete, glacial *Perseus* stands out like architecture against the cool gray columns that line the walls of this monumental staircase. You have to admire the elegant monochrome of the different marbles as you look across the central void. And from directly opposite there comes a surprise, a burst of color from the great Tiepolo in the gallery beyond.

TOMB FIGURE

Traces of painting on hard clay,

China, Han Dynasty (206 B.C.–220 A.D.)

Purchase, Rogers Fund, 1920 (20.39.1)

THIS SIMPLE FIGURINE IN TERRA-COTTA
was not made for the delectation of connoisseurs—it pre-
dates the aesthetic tradition in Far Eastern art by many
centuries. The ancient Chinese made careful prepara-
tions for the burial of their dead, and during the Han
dynasty a wide variety of small clay sculptures of people
and animals, called *ming-ch'i*, were deposited in tombs
for use in the afterlife. Their special function was to
wait—and this plain figure is the embodiment of patient
attendance. Although this representation of a mere mor-
tal does not have the overt religiosity of the Nepalese
divinity that we have just seen (No. 37), it has an undeni-
able spiritual dimension. The torso is carefully described
to leave no doubt as to the purpose and costume of this
little person, but the lower body is hardly articulated at
all. The sculptor did not permit any trace of assertive
individuality to disturb the placid containment of this
devoted soul.

STATUETTE OF MAN

Copper, Iraq, Sumerian, about 2700 B.C.

Harris Brisbane Dick Fund, 1955 (55.142)

SUMER IS A PLACE THAT WAS: AN EARLY stopover along the road of civilization. This little man is an envoy from that almost forgotten past. He strides confidently into the twentieth century with well over 4,000 years of experience and testimony behind him. He is a time capsule who testifies that the making of art is inseparable from the definition of human culture. Why the Sumerians made him, we cannot say. The copper for this statuette was a precious material in metal-poor Mesopotamia. Supple and erect, unbowed by his burden, our little man has an air of readiness. His work is humble, but I admire the self-confidence with which he proceeds—it is clear that the sculptor who made him had respect for him. The same Sumerians created a time capsule in literature: *Gilgamesh*, the earliest known epic, whose hero was also, remarkably, a man rather than a god.

SEATED GUDEA

Diorite, Neo-Sumerian, about 2100 B.C.

Harris Brisbane Dick Fund, 1959 (59.2)

THIS SUMERIAN DESPOT, GUDEA, HAS
the self-conscious dignity of a pious autocrat: he had himself portrayed as simultaneously reverential and authori-
tative. The pose, costume, and features of the sculptured
effigies of Gudea and his son, Ur-Ningirsu, were pre-
scribed by fiat and endlessly repeated. The effort paid off,
and has brought this family a sort of immortality: Gudea
statues are found in museums all over the world. However
plentiful, these compact sculptures are consistently
impressive, and all in all they represent an artistic/reli-
gious program of remarkable ambition. This Gudea is
exceptional in that it retains its original head; the heads
and torsos of these statues are almost never preserved
together. These portraits must have seemed magical in
their time, because the Gudeas' resentful successors took
the trouble to knock off nearly all their heads. I cannot
imagine a more sincere tribute to their artistry.

BOWL

Earthenware, glazed, Islamic or Iranian, 10th c.

Rogers Fund, 1965 (65.106.2)

TOUR II
42

PERHAPS BECAUSE I CANNOT READ A
letter of the inscription on this bowl, it never occurs to me
that what I am enjoying here is the so-called art of callig-
raphy. Ornate handwriting seems to me a kind of craft, as
amusing as it often is. Here, however, there is an unmis-
takable seriousness to the undertaking that resulted in
this white bowl marked with Arabic script. The script
forms an elegant black-and-white pattern of the sort that
leaves an afterimage on the retina, and I find it more conducive to brainstorming (and infinitely more satisfying)
than a Rorschach test. Do the vertical strokes of these letters most resemble the spokes around a wheel, or pointing
fingers, or just drips of paint running into the bowl? Is the
solitary loop at the lower right a hieroglyph for love?
There are no incorrect answers to this quiz. The Met's own
Guide provides a translation of the inscription around the
rim, which consists of two seemingly unrelated messages:
"Planning before work protects you from regret; prosperity and peace."

111

PANATHENAIC

PRIZE AMPHORA

Terra-cotta, Greek (Attica), about 530 B.C.

Rogers Fund, 1914 (14.130.12)

THERE IS A GREAT PAINTING ON THE
side of this antique vase: a footrace among powerful men
who strain to go faster. The Greeks made art as an offering
at the temple of human beauty. From the Egyptians they inherited a curious way of drawing the figure—
the torso seen frontally, the head and limbs in profile. I
suspect that they were loath to omit any part of something
that seemed so beautiful. The Greeks drew more delicately than the Egyptians, however, and their paintings
have an elegance to which the practical Egyptians did not
aspire. The scope of the Met's collection of Greek vases is
admittedly a little daunting. I suggest this amphora as a
good point of departure. The tracing of the musculature is
admirably refined, but even more distinctive is the suc-
cess with which this anonymous painter has conveyed the
excitement of the event. Red, black, red, black—our
painter has created a visual rhythm of heads, arms, and
legs that fills our eyes and ears with the shouting, thrust-
ing, pounding of a footrace twenty-five centuries ago. The
winner took home this amphora, the original trophy cup.

STUDY IN THE NUDE

FOR THE DRESSED

BALLET DANCER

Bronze, after a model by Edgar Degas (1834–1917)

Bequest of Mrs. H. O. Havemeyer, 1929. The H. O. Havemeyer

Collection (29.100.373)

114

THE WHOLE RANGE OF DEGAS'S EXPRES-
sion is encapsulated in this bronze, an anatomical study.
He dressed the final version of this brittle little girl in a
cloth tutu, which caused a sensation because of its hyperrealism. The costumed ballerina (the Met owns a cast)
remains a perennial favorite. But the nude study strikes
me as infinitely more disturbing: it is an unblinking rendition of prepubescent awkwardness. The peculiar
genius of Degas lies in his reticence. He withholds any
judgment. Is she beautiful or ugly? Degas seems to say
that the facts of life do not conform to aesthetic catego-
ries. All we are left with are the facts. This child seems to
have a thousand tiny bones like a bird, and to be every bit
as fragile. She tries to put on a grown-up pout, but her
spindly thighs and skinny chest belie the attempt. She
stands with the practiced poise of a dancer, but her childish innocence gives her away.

NIJINSKY

Bronze, by Auguste Rodin, 1912

Private Collection (L.1979.76)

IN THE EXTENSIVE ICONOGRAPHY OF the great dancer Vaslav Nijinsky, this small bronze is unsurpassed. Nijinsky redefined the terms of modern dance, and only Rodin has come close to conveying his intensity and inner force. Coiled in readiness to leap, the dancer is caught at the instant of his explosive propulsion into space. Rodin saw Nijinsky perform in his sensational "Afternoon of a Faun," and he immediately sought to sculpt him. Nijinsky posed in the nude for Rodin in 1912; the dancer and the sculptor worked through the night to perfect the model for this extraordinary portrait. It is said that Diaghilev, Nijinsky's jealous impresario, stalked furiously out of the studio.

INVITATION TO THE
SIDE-SHOW (<u>LA PARADE</u>)

Oil on canvas, by Georges Seurat, 1887–1888

Bequest of Stephen C. Clark, 1960 (61.101.17)

GEORGES SEURAT LIKED TO APPLY HIS paints in dots or commas (Pointillism) and not in strokes, as every other painter had done since the caves in Lascaux. He had a theory about color enhancement that required him to juxtapose complementary colors; blue and orange appear constantly in this way. Seurat had a dozen such theories that even art historians are still hard put to understand. Upward curves are happy, he observed, so when he painted a circus scene (now in Paris), he made everyone, everything, point furiously to the sky. Seurat composed this painting of a sideshow orchestra with the same extraordinary single-mindedness. This time, though, curves and circles—anything nonrectilinear—have been rigorously banished. It makes an odd impression, if you think about it, because strictly horizontal and vertical accents are the time-hallowed hallmarks of classical harmony and balance. Another Frenchman of two centuries earlier, Nicolas Poussin, would have admired the subtlety with which the background of Seurat's painting is organized into interlocking rectangles. Yet the oppressive shadows and the eerie, greasy light of the gas lamps imbue this street scene with the murky aura of an underworld. The soloist rises isolated on the central block, an inscrutable sphinx. At right, the master of these ceremonies struts onto the stage. There's no telling what the next entertainment will be, so I suggest that we not linger too long.

MARGOT BÉRARD

Oil on canvas, by Pierre Auguste Renoir, 1879

Bequest of Stephen C. Clark, 1960 (61.101.15)

120

RENOIR NEVER PAINTED A BETTER
picture than this. To give him due credit, he painted some
very good ones that are larger and that made him
famous—boating parties, family groups, dancing
alfresco—but the spontaneity, intimacy, and goodwill of
this small study are unmatched. The problem with Renoir
is always excess—too many paintings, too decorative,
too quickly done—but this portrait of Margot Bérard
dates from his best period and leaves us begging to know
more about this delightful girl. She was the daughter of a
good friend, and Renoir paid his respects with one of the
most engaging portraits of a child in art.

THE ENGLISHMAN
AT THE MOULIN ROUGE

Oil and gouache on cardboard, by Henri de Toulouse-Lautrec, 1892

Bequest of Miss Adelaide Milton de Groot (1876–1967),

1967 (67.187.108)

HERE A JAUNTY ENGLISHMAN, WITH HIS
topper and inevitable gold-headed cane and gloves,
engages two ladies of the evening in animated discourse
with the intent to engage one, or both, in a more meaning-
ful and physical dialogue. Lautrec had the special genius
both to isolate and to contain this lascivious gent within
the frame of his semierotic behavior. The Prince of Wales,
Oscar Wilde, and all the Russians of royal blood came
into the Moulin Rouge, the most popular hangout for the
Parisian demimonde. Lautrec, an insider who viewed the
scene with witty detachment, drew them all. This painting was copied in a poster, an art form at which Lautrec
excelled, and his subject, a failed English artist, had the
dubious distinction of being plastered *tout Paris*.

PEPITO COSTA Y BONELLS

Oil on canvas, by Francisco Goya, about 1810

Gift of Countess Bismarck, 1961 (61.259)

The MET HAS TWO PORTRAITS BY GOYA
of solemn little boys. One, the red-suited Don Manuel
Osorio, is probably the most famous single painting in the
museum—you'll look at it anyway. I love the Osorio, but
lately I gravitate more and more to the more natural
Pepito, painted later in Goya's life. Almost a quarter of a
century passed between the two works, in which time
Goya's illness worsened, his romance with Alba with-
ered, and Spain was ravaged by war. Works of art should
be judged in isolation from their creators' biographies,
but I cannot help sensing a very different psychology
behind these two pictures. In the earlier portrait, Goya's
attention is divided between Don Manuel and his pets:
the intrigue between cats and bird is everybody's favorite
part and is thought to have symbolic overtones. Pepito is
also surrounded by props: his toys and even his jacket
and haircut are allusions to the impact of Napoleon. Yet
Pepito retains his individuality in a way that Don Manuel
does not. His sad, serious stare is the essence of this
painting. I am conscious, looking into his face, that
Pepito was a (little) person who really was, not a stand-in
for a philosophical argument.

THE WHALE SHIP

Oil on canvas, by J. M. W. Turner (1775–1851)

Wolfe Fund, 1896, Catharine Lorillard Wolfe Collection (96.29)

WHEN FACED WITH ABSTRACT OR NEARLY abstract painting, I find it helpful to ask myself what the artist has actually given us to see. Titles were very important to Turner, because they allowed him to skip the narration and get on with the music. This painting is about men who are experiencing extreme anxiety, who are caught up in circumstances beyond their control. The whale ship is a metaphor. I remember that it was for Melville too. As I look into this tempest, one by one the forms dissolve. I see three boats, but there are no faces; there are not even any men. At left there is no whale to be seen, there is only a black patch. I see the sails of a ship, but there is no ship. I hear water pounding, men screaming, and I can taste the saltwater spray. The late paintings by Turner have been celebrated in recent years as antecedents to the Abstract Expressionism of the New York School. Twenty years ago the Museum of Modern Art organized an exhibition of these pictures—not bad for a painter who died in 1851. Turner and Constable were the paragons of Romantic painting in England, and both artists (Constable in his sketches especially) regarded the randomness and the ceaseless variety of natural phenomena as metaphors for the unfathomable depths of the human soul.

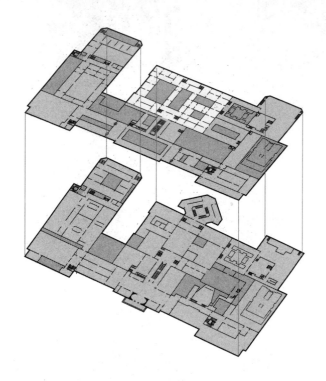

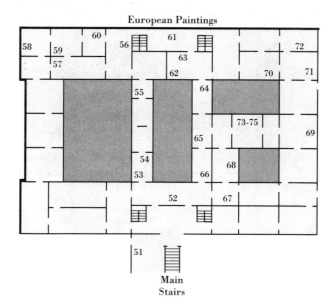

European Paintings

58
59
57
60
56
61
63
62
72
70
71
55
54
53
64
65
66
68
73-75
69
52
67
51

Main
Stairs

SECOND FLOOR,
CHINESE AND EUROPEAN PAINTINGS

51. White Vase. Porcelain. (1723.1736).

● *European Paintings*

52. The Farnese Table. Designed by Jacopo Barozzi da Vignola. (58.57 a-d).

53. Portrait of a Carthusian. Petrus Christus. (49.7.19).

54. Portrait of a Man. Hugo van der Goes. (29.100.15).

55. Portrait of a Man in a Red Cap. Hans Holbein the Younger. (50.145.24).

56. Lucas Van Uffele. Anthony van Dyck. (14.40.619).

57. The Holy Family with Saints Anne and Catherine of Alexandria. Jusepe Ribera. (34.73).

58. Juan de Pareja. Diego Velázquez. (1971.86).

59. The Virgin and Child. Bartolomé Esteban Murillo. (43.13).

60. Study Head of a Young Woman. Anthony van Dyck. (57.37).

61. Portrait of a Young Man. Bronzino. (29.100.16).

62. Three Miracles of Saint Zenobius. Alessandro Botticelli. (11.98).

63. The Young Saint John the Baptist. Piero di Cosimo. (22.60.52).

64. Madonna and Child. Carlo Crivelli. (49.7.5).

65. Portrait of a Man and a Woman at a Casement. Fra Filippo Lippi. (89.15.19).

66. Saint Andrew. Simone Martini. (41.100.23).

67. Mezzetin. Jean Antoine Watteau. (34.138).

68. A Dance in the Country. Giovanni Domenico Tiepolo. (1980.67).

69. Lady with a Pink. Rembrandt van Rijn. (14.40.622).

70. The Companions of Rinaldo. Nicolas Poussin. (1977.1.2).

71. Young Woman with a Water Jug. Joannes Vermeer. (89.15.21).

72. The Crucifixion with the Virgin and Saint John. Hendrick Terbrugghen. (56.228).

● *Altman Collection*

73. Young Saint John the Baptist. Mino da Fiesole. (14.40.688).

74. Madonna and Child with Angels. Antonio Rosellino. (14.40.675).

75. Madonna and Child with Scroll. Luca della Robbia. (14.40.685).

WHITE VASE

Porcelain, Chinese, Yung-Ch'ing Dynasty, 1723–1736 (14.40.140)

The Altman Collection, 1914

TOUR III
51

L IKE THE "CLEANSING BREATH" BEFORE
meditation, a pause in front of this pure white porcelain
will ready us for the sensory richness of the Old Masters
that follow in this tour. If you are coming from the nine-
teenth-century paintings in the André Meyer Galleries, I
suggest you use this vase as a sorbet for your eyes, something to clear your palate between courses. The finest
Chinese porcelains are exercises in chaste form, metaphors for the Absolute. Somewhere on this silken surface
a dragon is incised so delicately as to seem more illusion
than decoration. The curves and volumes are something
nameless, neither sensuous nor geometric. This is the
kind of sculpture they have in Heaven, carved from cloud
and glazed with white air.

THE FARNESE TABLE

Marble, alabaster, and semiprecious stones,

designed by Jacopo Barozzi da Vignola, about 1565–1573

Harris Brisbane Dick Fund, 1958 (58.57 a-d)

Big as it is, very few people stop to look at this table (unless they happen to back into it). In the Farnese Palace in Rome this marble tour de force was so conspicuous that it gave its name to the room in which it stood. The scale, design, and detail of the Metropolitan are palatial to be sure, but in addition to paintings on the walls, a Renaissance palazzo was richly furnished with noble and lovingly crafted chairs, beds, cassoni, and tables. Nobody lives like that anymore, and mass-produced dinette sets make it hard for us to see furniture as art. On this table rare marbles and semiprecious stones sumptuously frame the two vast slabs of alabaster. The tabletop rests like a huge slice of plum cake on three massive marble piers alive with grotesques. When the cardinals and princes of the Farnese house assembled around this table, they must have enjoyed the feel under their fingertips of this concrete symbol of their own substance, taste, and status. Jacopo da Vignola, who designed the Farnese table, was the greatest architect of the late sixteenth century: this piece exemplifies the curious aesthetics of that time. On the one hand, fantasy and an infatuation with luxury, even ostentation, were the orders of the day. On the other hand, these excesses were intentionally blunted—and Vignola was the best at this—through their containment in immutable patterns of the most excruciating geometric perfection.

PORTRAIT

OF A CARTHUSIAN

Tempera and oil on wood, by Petrus Christus, 1446

Jules Bache Collection, 1949 (49.7.19)

This youngish man with his extraordinary beard wears the brilliant white habit of the Carthusian order. The contrast between his robe and the scarlet backdrop makes a strong impression even from a distance, despite the size of this miniature (or near miniature) portrait. I doubt that the halo is original—the man seems too involved with our earthly world to qualify for sainthood. At a later date, some collector (or dealer) must have responded to the intelligence and self-assurance in his face and arranged an impromptu canonization. Seemingly so subtle, the halo severely compromises the integrity of the artist's composition. Without it, the expressive head of this monk would fill the niche in which he sits. As it is, the halo's arc tends to focus our attention on this noble head in isolation from his shoulders. The outsize fly on the parapet merits a footnote. Petrus Christus, distinguished pupil of Jan van Eyck, indulged himself a bit with this detail. A symbol of vanitas, is this fly part of the Carthusian's space or ours? Could it be a fly that has lit on the painted sill, deceived by the power of art? Well satisfied with his work, Christus carved his signature and the date into the same piece of feigned stone: it says, *Petrus* XPI [Christi] ME FECIT *Ao 1446*.

PORTRAIT OF A MAN

Tempera and oil on wood, Hugo van der Goes, about 1470

Bequest of Mrs. H. O. Havemeyer, 1929, The H. O. Havemeyer Collection (29.100.15)

AFTER THE EXOTICISM OF CHRISTUS'S Carthusian, this young man by Hugo van der Goes is reassuring for his calm familiarity. Maybe you know somebody who looks like him: could you say that of the Carthusian? These two portraits, considered together, make an interesting statement about realism. Why does the man painted by van der Goes appear more lifelike? A minute ago, the Carthusian monk seemed the last word in this department: Christus recorded every detail with uncompromising precision. But the result is a kind of hyperrealism, providing more visual minutiae than our eyes are capable of absorbing. Van der Goes made accommodations to the limitations of sight. The stubble of this man's beard, for example, is rendered as a shadowy tone, quite unlike the prickly web of the Carthusian. And it is closer, finally, to natural appearances. To a certain extent, this development can be credited to the advances shared by a younger generation of painters, but even in his day van der Goes was renowned as an outstanding naturalist. This portrait was later cut down to an oval from its original rectangle: the most provocative works of art often suffer the worst indignities. The window at the lower right is mostly restoration.

PORTRAIT OF A

MAN IN A RED CAP

Tempera and oil on wood, by Hans Holbein the Younger, about 1535

Bequest of Mary Stillman Harkness, 1950 (50.145.24)

THE MET OWNS TWO FINE PAINTINGS by Holbein—this little roundel is the one everybody overlooks. Modern art has conditioned us to value paintings in proportion to their size (large pictures are "museum scale," small ones are not) and to their suitability for attachment to a wall. We hardly have the patience to look through the contents of a glassed-in case, and we certainly don't expect to find a Holbein there. In the Renaissance and earlier the outlook was different: artistic importance was related to excellence, and small was more likely to mean precious than insignificant. For Holbein miniature painting was an expansion not a limitation of his genius, another forum for virtuosity. This stolid young man with a tuberous nose sits diffidently for his portrait. He wears the red cap and jacket insignia of an attendant at the court of the redoubtable Henry VIII. Holbein painted other circular portraits on wooden panels, and some of these—maybe this one too—were originally intended for display inside the lids of carved and gilt boxes.

LUCAS VAN UFFELE

Oil on canvas, by Anthony Van Dyck, about 1622

Bequest of Benjamin Altman, 1913 (14.40.619)

Van Dyck is the quintessential portrait painter of status. His icons of European aristocracy stand shoulder to shoulder in the marble corridors of every American museum, as testimony to the taste of American industrialist collectors at the turn of the twentieth century. The Frick Collection has a Genoese noblewoman and Sir John Suckling; in Washington, the National Gallery has rooms full of such pictures—great ones. The Met also has a superb portrait of James Stewart at ease with his hound. The Met also has this painting of van Uffele, a Flemish merchant and art collector living in Venice, which offers a refreshing departure from genteel passivity and every-hair-in-place. Like other Van Dyck subjects, this man wears the semi-smile of self-assurance. Unlike the others, *Lucas van Uffele* is an image of flux—not in a social sense (naturally not) but in terms of physical action. Van Dyck painted van Uffele as a man who hadn't the time to sit for his portrait. His hand pushes down on the chair arm, and he pulls away from the table. Before him lie various attributes of his learning and taste. Van Dyck has ingeniously contrasted the active and intellectual temperaments of Lucas van Uffele, businessman and connoisseur.

THE HOLY FAMILY
WITH SAINTS ANNE AND
CATHERINE OF ALEXANDRIA

Oil on canvas, by Jusepe Ribera, 1648

Samuel D. Lee Fund, 1934 (34.73)

RIBERA PAINTED GRAND COMPOSITIONS
which, paradoxically, are best appreciated from close up.
His canvases were brushed with a fluency and rapidity
that made him the envy of every Italian virtuoso. At the
same time Ribera's brushstrokes seem in some uncanny
way to represent the fine lines or fibers in the flesh or fab-
ric that he was depicting. This is easiest to see in the
wrinkles of Saint Anne's face and hand, but in every pas-
sage of his work, Ribera's brushwork and its ceaseless
shifts and changes are crucial to the final effect of illusion. A Spaniard who spent his whole artistic life in
Naples, Ribera has been called the most realistic painter
who ever lived—quite a claim for a contemporary of
Velázquez and Rembrandt!

JUAN DE PAREJA

Oil on canvas, by Diego Velázquez, 1650

Fletcher Fund, Rogers Fund, and Bequest of Miss Adelaide

Milton de Groot (1876–1967), by exchange, supplemented

by gifts from friends of the Museum, 1971 (1971.86)

In 1650 VELÁZQUEZ, PAINTER TO THE King of Spain, was in Rome, and he sent this painting to an open-air exhibition as a demonstration of his capabilities. The work caused a sensation for its astounding likeness—the feature that means least to us today. The most surprising thing about this portrait is the fact that it was painted at all. Velázquez was a court painter; his usual subjects in Madrid were noblemen and favorites of the king. Juan de Pareja was a slave. That Velázquez, who hoped to paint the pope during his visit to Rome, should decide to exhibit a portrait of his slave was exceptional enough. But imagine the reaction of a seventeenth-century audience when they saw Pareja, a Moor, depicted with all the dignity and self-possession of a Venetian doge. He is dressed without pretension, yet he is at ease in a pose inspired by Titian.

THE VIRGIN AND CHILD

Oil on canvas, by Bartolomé Esteban Murillo, about 1670

Rogers Fund, 1943 (43.13)

As SWEET AND PURE AS SPRING WATER
this Madonna represents an ideal that is more foreign to
our taste than the Gothic extravagance of a Virgin by Van
Eyck. Murillo's art came into being in direct response to
the religious issues of his time, the Spanish Baroque,
when the civic life of Seville was saturated with devotional concerns, when theology, not politics, brought
crowds of citizens into the streets. Murillo is often
accused of being sentimental—certainly the naturalness
and mutual love of this Virgin and Child are not calcu-
lated to harden our hearts. His art rises far above surface
emotions, however; I see it as an expression of unques-
tioning, unqualified faith. Murillo drew inspiration from
two other masters: his near contemporary, Van Dyck, and
Raphael of the High Renaissance. From the former he
adopted the naturalism and tangible atmosphere of
Baroque style. From Raphael, Murillo derived the monumental simplicity of pose and the sense of innate nobility
of this mother and child, who are in but not of our world.

STUDY HEAD

OF A YOUNG WOMAN

Oil on paper, mounted on wood, by Anthony van Dyck (1599–1641)

Gift of Mrs. Ralph J. Hines, 1957 (57.37)

My FAVORITE PAINTING IN THIS GALLERY is by far the least spectacular: this simple oil study of a young woman's head and languorous hair. Van Dyck learned from his master, Rubens, the practice of making oil sketches as preparatory research for his finished works. Van Dyck's sketches for complete compositions are admirable for their freedom and liveliness; his studies of heads, for example this one, are always impressive for their naturalness. Something sets this particular sketch apart, however: it seems complete within itself, not a fragment of a larger idea. This beautiful, intelligent young woman draws her head back in rapture—we wonder why. Her long, smooth throat is revealed, and her fine hair trails behind her in a slow, unending curve. Her emotions remain strictly private. In the mid-nineteenth century the Pre-Raphaelite Dante Gabriel Rossetti painted heads strikingly similar to this one as he sought to depict an impossibly elusive ideal of feminine grace. He could have profited from Van Dyck's example and made nature, not philosophy, his point of departure.

PORTRAIT OF A YOUNG MAN

Oil on wood, by Bronzino, about 1540

Bequest of Mrs. H. O. Havemeyer, H. O. Havemeyer Collection,

1929 (29.100.16)

A GREAT PORTRAITIST HAS TO BE A genius, because he has to describe somebody else's emotions and intelligence without losing himself in the process. Any Sunday painter can get the nose and eyes right. I admire the self-assurance of this young man. Certainly he is well turned out, but his elegance is not a result of his dress. Actually his poise makes his black suit appear fancy, and not vice versa. But his arms and hands are self-consciously graceful, so how does this effete young man in a curious cap avoid looking like a fool? The answer is in his eyes. He has this extraordinary gaze. With one eye he looks directly at you; his other eye seems to look at something rather more interesting. I doubt that this handsome aristocrat was able to use his eyes in this way any more than you or I can. Fortunately for him he had access to Bronzino, the smartest portraitist in Florence during the late Renaissance.

Bronzino was roughly the contemporary of Titian in Venice, and much as Titian was able to portray people in their natural aspects, Bronzino was able to invent qualities for his sitters that they may or may not have actually possessed. Typical of Bronzino's approach is the cubistic room that is the backdrop for this portrait. To me the room looks impenetrable, with jutting walls and partially seen pieces of furniture barring the way. The young man, however, has a total command of this inhospitable place; he looks like a giant, taller than the door.

THREE MIRACLES

OF SAINT ZENOBIUS

Tempera on wood, by Alessandro Botticelli, about 1500

John Stewart Kennedy Fund, 1911 (11.98)

DOWNSTAIRS IN THE ROBERT LEHMAN Collection, the small painting of *The Annunciation* (No. 19) revealed Botticelli in his guise as Renaissance mathematician. The Met also has an extraordinary panel by Botticelli the mystic. Called upon to depict scenes from the life of Saint Zenobius, Botticelli responded with medieval logic: from left to right, four distinct events transpire with apparent simultaneity in a nonexistent place. In the foreground of Botticelli's town of miracles, for example, Zenobius resurrects believers from the dead. The miracle at the far right is accomplished by a white-robed acolyte with water blessed by Zenobius (who is visible through the transparent wall in the distance). Like weightless spirits Botticelli's figures glide to and fro amid these forbidding facades. What lies at the end of this central avenue bordered by converging blocks of buildings? Botticelli's rendition of the supernatural is a dissertation on the surreal worthy of De Chirico.

THE YOUNG

SAINT JOHN THE BAPTIST

Oil and tempera on wood, by Piero di Cosimo (b.1462, d.1521?)

The Bequest of Michael Dreicer, 1921 (22.60.52)

IT IS HARD TO PUT INTO WORDS MY delight in this simple picture. Piero shows us so little: just the profile of a boy with golden, curly hair. A great artist can afford to dispense character in teaspoonfuls—his draftsmanship is that potent. The cruciform staff identifies this child as the young John the Baptist. Doesn't he seem too placid to be an ascetic in training? True enough, Renaissance Florence took particular consolation in the essential humanity of its patron saint. But Piero's subject is rather more than an amiable *ragazzo*. Almost all his expression is concentrated around the eye: the wrinkles of the lower lid are somehow unmistakably the sign of an honest, open heart. His high brow is proof of his intelligence. This firm, strong mouth could only speak the truth. Does it seem overly subtle to read a painting line by line in this way? Nonetheless, it often happens in art that the greatest masters assume from us as audience a certain confidence in their powers, a faith that the meaning of their work derives from their inspired design and not merely from happy accident.

MADONNA AND CHILD

Tempera and gold on wood, by Carlo Crivelli, about 1480

The Jules Bache Collection, 1949 (49.7.5)

I LIKE THIS LITTLE PICTURE FOR ITS sheer obstinacy. Crivelli was an obstinate artist who stuck to an idiosyncratic style that is both instantly recognizable and an acquired taste. On the eve of the High Renaissance, Crivelli continued to paint spiky compositions, bristling with thorns and Gothic pinnacles. While his Venetian contemporaries experimented with oils, Crivelli doggedly pursued the slow, meticulous technique of tempera. On the other hand, Crivelli was also determined to prove that he was up-to-date. The Child makes that grimace just to show that Crivelli could match Mantegna in difficult foreshortening. Those giant peaches drop from the sky and prove that, again from Mantegna, our artist had learned about similar garlands in ancient art. I wonder whether Crivelli was trying to paint a religious picture or a still life. True, the goldfinch, fly, and fruits are encoded references to sin and redemption, but aren't they supposed to be subsidiary to the figures? Crivelli always took pains to make his apples and cucumbers as natural as they could be, and he has often been regarded as a sort of precursor to still life painting (which did not come into independent existence for fully a hundred years). In the end Crivelli did it his way and managed to carve his niche in the history books.

PORTRAIT OF A MAN AND
A WOMAN AT A CASEMENT

Tempera on wood, by Fra Filippo Lippi, about 1440

Gift of Henry G. Marquand, 1889 (89.15.19)

This PORTRAIT BY FRA FILIPPO LIPPI would be handsome and otherwise unremarkable if its subject were only the velvet-dressed lady in half-length. The proportions of her figure are perfectly consistent with the rectangular format of the painting. But Lippi, for reasons that remain unfathomable, proceeded to construct a closet-sized room for his lady and then introduce a friend peeping in at the window. He stares intently at her nose, I suppose, because he appears deeper in space, yet his head is about the same size as hers. The central window gives onto a garden at some distance below: is the gentleman caller standing on a balcony or clinging to the sill for dear life? Maybe the lady has stopped in front of and is blocking the subject of a different painting altogether. Perspectival ambiguities like this should have been anathema to a faithful pupil of Masaccio (who never painted a picture without a stylus and straightedge). Double portraits of men and women were often commissioned in association with weddings. And if such was the case here, unless the engagement was announced after Lippi had already completed two-thirds of his portrait of the future bride, I am at a loss to explain how this marriage started off on such unequal footing.

SAINT ANDREW

Tempera and gold on wood, by Simone Martini, about 1325

Gift of George Blumenthal, 1941 (41.100.23)

F OR YEARS THIS FIGURE OF SAINT
Andrew was attributed to a lesser painter, Lippo Vanni.
But for once an attribution was upgraded. Simone Martini
is perhaps not a household name, but the fault lies in ourselves. The scion of Sienese painting in the mid-four-
teenth century, Simone achieved a delicacy of outline,
not to mention sentiment, that stood up proudly against
the revolutionary realism forged by Giotto in Florence. A
saint shown in half-length, holding a book—for most
people today this seems dry going indeed. Simone's mastery emerges most readily in his rendering of textures.
When Simone painted hands, the skin became demon-
strably smooth and taut; Saint Andrew's beard bristles
like wire. This is the moment of transition from Gothic to
Renaissance: a vision of divinity that does not preclude a
receptive response to nature. The sad truth is that our
appreciation of gold-ground paintings is made more difficult by the fact that few of them can be seen in American
museums in anything like their original contexts. These
saints and angels in their curiously shaped frames were
all created as facets of grand, shining, carved and gilt
ensembles that have long since been dismembered. Our
Saint Andrew turns to pay homage to a Madonna and
Child who, by happy coincidence, can be visited downstairs in the Robert Lehman Collection, together with
another worshiper from the same altarpiece, Saint
Ansanus.

MEZZETIN

Oil on canvas, by Jean Antoine Watteau, about 1718

Munsey Fund, 1934 (34.138)

164

THE GUIDEBOOKS CAN TELL YOU THAT this fellow, Mezzetin (roughly, "half-pint"), was a comic character in the improvisatory commedia dell'arte of the eighteenth century and earlier. He is dressed in outlandish stripes, and his cap looks like a mop, but I doubt that Watteau was trying to make me laugh. Actually, it is hard to say what Watteau was trying to do in his art. More than any other artist he invented the lighthearted style of eighteenth-century French painting. He painted theatrical companies, garden parties, and boudoirs. His pupils, Lancret and Pater, copied his colors and extracted every trace of *joie de vivre* that they could find. Ironically, however, the greatness of Watteau lies in his *tristesse*. His paintings are melancholy, like the memory of a dream. No one after him, not Boucher or Fragonard, made the slightest attempt to imitate Watteau in this. Mezzetin was unlucky in love, and on the stage he was an easy target for buffoonery. Watteau shows us that Mezzetin tries too hard; he throws his head back in an unpersuasive croon. Even the garden statuary turns its back to him—a good joke at Mezzetin's expense. Why then don't we laugh? Because Watteau's Mezzetin is not the straw man of the theater, he is individual and vulnerable. His face is probably the portrait of one of Watteau's friends. This *Mezzetin* is no more funny than the times in our lives when we have loved without being loved in return.

A DANCE IN THE COUNTRY

Oil on canvas, by Giovanni Domenico Tiepolo, about 1756

Gift of Mr. and Mrs. Charles Wrightsman, 1980 (1980.67)

Veteran museumgoers know that Tiepolo was the foremost painter of eighteenth-century Venice. At the top of the grand staircase, the Met has a whole roomful of huge Tiepolos emptied out of a Venetian palazzo. Look again, though, at the label under this *Dance in the Country*: Giovanni *Domenico* Tiepolo was the son of the famous Giovanni Battista Tiepolo. Until recently Domenico Tiepolo was considered only a waste bin for dubious attributions to his father. But a handful of paintings like this festive dance *alfresco* prove that he had distinct qualities and preferences of his own. Above all Domenico found joy in the liveliness of Venetian popular culture, in carnival escapades, and in the satiric theater of the commedia dell'arte. The splashy colors and fearless brushwork he learned from his father proved to be terrifically suited to lighthearted subjects like this carnival costume party. Battista Tiepolo painted the loves and wars of the Roman pantheon and would probably have felt faintly embarrassed to direct his fabled brush to some ordinary citizens kicking up their heels. Domenico, alas, did not do these vivacious subjects often enough to satisfy today's demand. The Met is fortunate to have recently been given one of his best.

LADY WITH A PINK

Oil on canvas, by Rembrandt van Rijn, about 1662–1665

Bequest of Benjamin Altman, 1913 (14.40.622)

THE LADY WITH A PINK IS ONE OF those great Rembrandts that always make me wonder exactly what the good burghers of Amsterdam could have made of the portraits that Rembrandt painted for them. The results were rather more than tintypes for the family album. The Dutch in their greatest century of prosperity were mad to have their portraits taken, and they supported a growth industry of painters. They invariably sat soberly and wore their richest clothes (or even costumes), and they were reasonably keen (as the French never were) to have their features recorded, warts and all. Although the story of Rembrandt's declining reputation has been romanticized into Hollywood melodrama, it is undeniably true that the old Rembrandt was no longer the portraitist of demand, as he had been in the 1630s. From our vantage point we can see that Rembrandt was willing to respect the prevailing conventions of portrait making, because nothing (not even somebody else's portrait) could distract him from his purpose, which was to paint pictures about *himself*. As far as I can see, this beautiful lady and her flower had no cause to complain. She came one day with her husband (his picture is adjacent) to sit for the famous and cantankerous Rembrandt. Her tired face is warmed by an inward spirituality. Whether the lady was as intelligent and contemplative as Rembrandt painted her we shall never know. It only matters that she inspired Rembrandt to make this unforgettable image of beauty imperiled by age.

THE COMPANIONS

OF RINALDO

Oil on canvas, by Nicolas Poussin, about 1630

Gift of Mr. and Mrs. Charles Wrightsman, 1977 (1977.1.2)

O VERLY ENTHUSIASTIC EMULATION of Classical statuary has led to some airless art, and even the great Poussin sometimes peopled his canvases with frozen figures. This early work by Poussin, however, is a full-blooded scene of manly action. The two soldiers stride forthrightly into the jaws of danger: a dragon, whose serpentine coils are dimly glimpsed at the edge of the painting. The story comes from the favorite adventure yarn of the seventeenth century: the epic *Jerusalem Delivered* by the Italian poet Tasso. It doesn't take a philologist to recognize that these knights (dressed in full Roman regalia, as was Poussin's wont) are good, while their adversary is in the service of Evil. Their captain, Rinaldo, has been bewitched by a comely sorceress in an enchanted garden, and these no-nonsense lads have to dispatch the dragon before proceeding to Rinaldo's rescue. Waiting in the wings was the First Crusade.

YOUNG WOMAN WITH
A WATER JUG

Oil on canvas, by Joannes Vermeer, about 1660

Gift of Henry G. Marquand, 1889 (89.15.21)

THE GENIUS OF ANY INTERIOR BY
Vermeer is simply that Vermeer tells us less. He does not
encumber our imaginations with useless facts. I don't
need to count the threads to know that the Oriental rug
is a good one. The pretty maiden pauses to look out the
window, but what does she see, and exactly what does she
intend to do with her brass pitcher and bowl? Dutch
painters worth their salt abhorred uncertainties like
these. Vermeer, a poet surrounded by chroniclers, tran-
scended the accepted conventions. In this painting he
made the background lighter than the foreground, which
was unusual for everyone except Vermeer, but he had to
do it this way—how else could he fix forever in our minds
the silhouette of this slender girl?

THE CRUCIFIXION WITH
THE VIRGIN AND SAINT JOHN

Oil on canvas, by Hendrick Terbrugghen, about 1620

Purchase, 1956, funds from various donors (56.228)

TOUR III
72

T ERBRUGGHEN PAINTED A CRUCIFIXION
like no other of the seventeenth century. It is a vision of
nobility and horror locked in unresolvable conflict. This
dichotomy lies at the root of the art of Terbrugghen, a
Dutchman who was formed in Italy under the influence of
Caravaggio and others. Terbrugghen's Crucifixion is a
Baroque picture infused with Gothic pathos: he has con-
sciously referred back to the art of an earlier century, spe-
cifically to the grimly expressive works of the German
Matthias Grünewald. The monumental simplicity and
equilibrium of Terbrugghen's composition, the exclusion
of every witness except the stars, and the ponderous,
sculptural drapery are all motifs of emotional reserve that
are abruptly dismissed by the apparition of the tortured
body on the cross and the blood that rains to the ground.

YOUNG SAINT JOHN

THE BAPTIST

Marble, by Mino da Fiesole, before 1484

Bequest of Benjamin Altman, 1913 (14.40.688)

A FLORENTINE PORTRAIT BUST OF GOOD quality: this much someone with experience in Italian art could tell you from a distance. On second look, though, this attractive adolescent identifies himself through his unruly hair and rustic garb (camel skins stitched together) as John the Baptist, revered as one of the patron saints of Florence. Surely there is no real sense of asceticism about this attractive young man with his perfect complexion and bright, candid gaze, but remember that the Florentine Renaissance is perhaps best known for its secularism. Mino da Fiesole specialized in portrait busts and in busts representing John the Baptist or Christ, and it appears that he was satisfied to interpret the secular and the saintly in remarkably similar terms. The holiness of the Baptist seems merely an expression of his superior humanity. In other works Mino attributed the same quality to the Florentine nobility, who took rather, more care, though, with their attire.

MADONNA AND
CHILD WITH ANGELS

Marble, by Antonio Rosellino, about 1460

Bequest of Benjamin Altman, 1913 (14.40.675)

Two emotions stir side by side in this marble, as though the sculptor did not wish to give primacy to any single interpretation. Seated on his mother's lap, the Child turns his body and faces outward with a confidence unexpected in an infant. His little arms seem strong and sure. By contrast, the almond-eyed Madonna—herself a young woman—bows her head pensively. He is ready to undertake his mission; she contemplates the sacrifice he must make. Florence during the 1400s was itself a culture divided between practicality and mysticism. The sculptor Rossellino was one of the most spiritual of artists; this relief is one of the finest early Renaissance works in America. The marble has a café-au-lait tint, the mottling of which contributes magically to the illusion of skin tone. As the Madonna gently extends her hand to embrace her Child, the veining in the stone seems to pulse with the warmth of human life.

MADONNA AND CHILD
WITH SCROLL

Enameled terra-cotta, by Luca della Robbia (b.1399 or 1400, d. 1482)

Bequest of Benjamin Altman, 1913 (14.40.685)

TOUR III
75

THIS CHOICE IS SHORT ON SNOB APPEAL.
The polychrome sculptures of the della Robbia family have fostered more collector's plates and garden wall decorations than the Statue of Liberty. The sad effect has been to discredit thoroughly the extraordinarily effective contrast of celestial blue and lead white. If snobbism is truly your concern, though, this can be your chance to outflank the opposition. Simply insist on the distinction between the original and the knockoff. The inventor of this style, Luca della Robbia, was a distinguished contemporary of Donatello, and the compositions traceable to him, such as this one, are unassailable achievements of the early Renaissance. They are by no means overly sentimental: Luca was a thorough classicist who understood the expressive power of restraint. And while we're at it, let's lay to rest another cliché: that these stuccos were made as cheap alternatives to marble statuary. Do they look like marble? Luca executed important commissions for polychrome terra-cottas, and everything indicates that his motivation was simply the desire to experiment with color. These polychromes were invariably intended for architectural contexts (in Brunelleschi designs, no less), and it still takes my breath away to see them set into the gray stone facades of Tuscany.

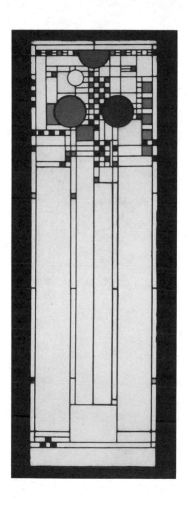

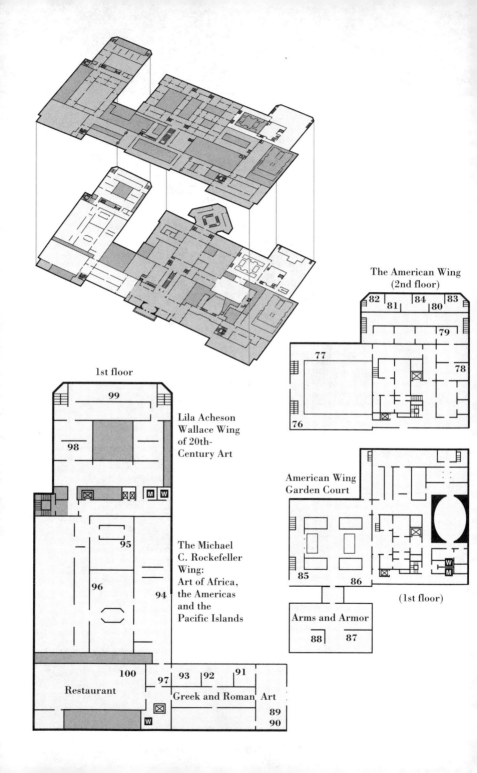

The American Wing
(2nd floor)

82 81 84 80 83

79

77

78

76

1st floor

99

98

Lila Acheson
Wallace Wing
of 20th-
Century Art

American Wing
Garden Court

95

The Michael
C. Rockefeller
Wing:
Art of Africa,
the Americas
and the
Pacific Islands

96

94

85 86

(1st floor)

Arms and Armor

88 87

100

97 93 92 91

Restaurant

Greek and Roman Art

89
90

AMERICAN WING, ARMS AND ARMOR, ROMAN, ROCKEFELLER WING, TWENTIETH-CENTURY WING

- *American Wing*

76. Vase. Louis Comfort Tiffany. (51.121.17).

77. Pair of Candlesticks. Isaac Hutton. (33.120.204–205).

78. Portrait Bust of Benjamin Franklin. Jean Antoine Houdon. (72.6).

79. Fur Traders Descending the Missouri. George Caleb Bingham. (33.61).

80. Still Life with Cake. Raphaelle Peale. (59.166).

81. Passing Away of the Storm. J. F. Kensett. (74.27).

82. Madame X. John Singer Sargent. (16.53).

83. Max Schmitt in a Single Scull. Thomas Eakins. (34.92).

84. Arques-la-Bataille. John H. Twachtman. (68.52).

85. Windows from the Avery Coonley Playhouse. Designed by Frank Lloyd Wright. (67.231.1–3).

86. Mantelpiece from the Vanderbilt House. By Augustus Saint-Gaudens, with mosaic designed by John La Farge. (25.234).

- *Arms and Armor*

87. Hilt of a Small Sword. (42.50.46).

88. Parade Helmet. Filippo Negroli. (17.190.1720).

- *Roman Art*

89. The Emperor Caligula. (14.37).

90. Urn in the Form of a Cylindrical Basket. (37.129a–b).

91. Statuette of a Warrior. (1972.118.53).

92. Statuette of an Athlete, The "Diadoumenos." (32.11.2).

93. Statuette of a Veiled Dancer. (1972.118.95).

- *Michael C. Rockefeller Wing*

94. Marionette. (1979.206.52).

95. Double-Headed Eagle Pendant. (1979.206.538).

96. Horn Blower. (1978.412.310).

97. Statuette of a Woman. (34.11.3).

- *Twentieth-Century Galleries*

98. Gertrude Stein. Pablo Picasso. (47.106).

99. I Saw the Figure 5 in Gold. Charles Demuth. (49.59.1).

100. History of Navigation, from the ocean liner *Normandie*. (1976.414.3).

VASE

Glass, by Louis Comfort Tiffany, late 19th c.

Gift of Louis Comfort Tiffany Foundation, 1951 (51.121.17)

Out OF ALL THE TIFFANY GLASSES in this amply crowded case, this tall, tapering vase is my favorite. Not that I would claim that its pattern is more shimmering and iridescent than its neighbors'. Or that this piece displays any better than these other works the marvelous fluidity of glass in its molten state. It's just that this exceptionally tall and thin vase seems to me like a comment on human folly. Ever since the invention of windows, baseballs, and boys, it has been universally recognized that the nature of glass is to be broken. How could anyone undertake to make a piece of glass so fragile, so impractical, as Tiffany did with this vase, and then how did Tiffany persuade someone else to buy it? In the end the whole process is a parable of optimism, and as of this writing the dream remains intact.

PAIR OF

CANDLESTICKS

Silver, by Isaac Hutton, c. 1800–1825

Bequest of A. T. Clearwater, 1933 (33.120.204–205)

Silver is a precious metal, but in a nonelectrified world, candlesticks were undeniably utilitarian. Americans have always prided themselves on their practicality, and during the Colonial and Federal periods, patronage of the best artisans was the most discreet way for a family to display its prosperity. Incalculably more patronage was expended to decorate the sideboard than on paintings for the walls. Unfortunately, silver is also readily convertible into ingots, and relatively few important silver candlesticks have been preserved. This pair by Hutton deserves a close look not for its scarcity, however, but for its craftsmanship and noble design. The early nineteenth century was wholly dedicated to the evocation of Classical art—Napoleon had found it the most suitable to his imperial ambitions. But much of Empire or Federal period art is outscaled and ungainly. It is especially satisfying to find pieces like these candlesticks that seem worthy of antiquity itself, so perfectly do they capture the restraint, lightness, and elegant proportions invented some 2,500 years ago.

PORTRAIT BUST OF

BENJAMIN FRANKLIN

Marble, by Jean Antoine Houdon, 1778

Gift of John Bard, 1872 (72.6)

A STRANGE FACE FOR A PERSONALITY who took the French by storm! The brilliance of Franklin's mind impressed them, of course, while his casualness of dress and demeanor left them breathless. The rumpled face of this wily old American launched a flood of popular images both in France and back home. For his part, the eminent Houdon raised Franklin iconography into the realm of High Art. Franklin's artlessness—his unkempt hair (no wig!) and simple dress—appear in piquant contrast to the complexity and canniness of his face. Houdon has treated the marble as if it were as malleable as clay and has underscored the telltale accidents of aging. At the same time the astute gaze and mobile expression (caught between a smile and a frown) emphasize this man's vigorous intelligence and ageless spirit.

FUR TRADERS DESCENDING
THE MISSOURI

Oil on canvas, by George Caleb Bingham, about 1845

Morris K. Jesup Fund, 1933 (33.61)

THE BACKBONE AND THE BANE OF
American painting is storytelling. Bingham specialized
in views of daily life along the Missouri River in the mid–
nineteenth century—so why hang his canvases in the
Met? Because he was more than a regional artist;
Bingham's reputation is based on two or three miraculous
paintings—this is one of them—in which he managed to
stop the action at a moment of perfect equilibrium. The
picture is arranged with all the geometry of a Mondrian.
The treetops make a line that cuts the canvas in half. But
the story keeps the scene from standing still. The day is
hot, humid, oppressive, and, for me, the air is heavy with
suspense. The boy seems happy enough for having shot a
waterfowl, yet the trader gives us a querulous look: he
fears for his cargo. Danger lies ahead. In the prow of the
canoe a fox sits like some apparition of the underworld.

STILL LIFE WITH CAKE

Oil on wood, by Raphaelle Peale (1774–1825)

Maria De Witt Jesup Fund, 1959 (59.166)

AMERICANS PRIDE THEMSELVES ON THEIR frankness and on their disinclination to make excuses for things being the way they are. It requires a distinctive set of mind for an artist to apply his hard-earned skills to the most faithful possible evocation of a raisin cake, as Peale has done here. The cake doesn't look fancy, but it must have been very good to eat. This picture is as uncontrived—and cogent—as the motto on a homespun sampler. Twenty years ago American still lifes were hardly appreciated, because the unassuming subject and unpretentious composition of the best ones were deemed embarrassing. The tide has surely turned now that a self-portrait (holding a pot of geraniums, for heaven's sake) by Rembrandt Peale, Raphaelle's bespectacled brother, has fetched a world's record price at auction. The Peales were the first dynasty of American painters, and they have not been greatly challenged since. The head of the family, Charles Willson Peale, was a well-known portraitist; he gave his sons the names of his favorite painters: Raphael, Rembrandt, Rubens, and Titian. The strange thing is that they all turned out to be pretty good painters.

PASSING AWAY OF THE STORM

Oil on canvas, by J. F. Kensett (1816–1872)

Gift of Thomas Kensett, 1874 (74.27)

Even WITHOUT THE TITLE, THE QUALITY of light in this little painting imbues it with an aura of aftermath and of tension that has been discharged into the air. The setting is still and dreamlike: Kensett has painted an elegy on the changing face of nature, the timelessness of landscape, and on the fragility of human existence in comparison to these. In this calm expanse of air and water, the role of mankind is like that of the tiny boats that drift placidly along the far horizon. Eventually they pass on, and others will take their place. It is not by coincidence that this picture alludes to Turner and anticipates the tonal unity favored by Whistler. In the 1840s Kensett traveled throughout Europe, then came home to filter the American landscape through a wide-angle, light-filled lens that ultimately links him to the Impressionists.

MADAME X

Oil on canvas, by John Singer Sargent, 1884

Purchase, Arthur H. Hearn Fund, 1916 (16.53)

WHAT A STUNNING PAINTING. IS IT *too* stagy to be a masterpiece? No matter, *Madame X* is one of the most arresting portraits in the Met. Sargent seems to have set out deliberately to make an icon of the Belle Epoque. Coming to New York and not looking at her would be like going to the Louvre and passing up the Mona Lisa. The subject is Madame Pierre Gautreau, a celebrated Parisian beauty (American-born) of the 1880s. Sargent has presented her in a long, black gown, in sharp profile. Her hair is coiffed tightly back, and her face is tinted lavender with makeup. Sargent's brushwork is uncharacteristically restrained and the background is suppressed, based on Velázquez. Although Sargent considered this picture "the best thing I have done," it was given a nasty reception at the Paris salon in 1884. Not surprisingly. Twenty years after Manet had painted the courtesan *Olympia* and been roundly denounced, the French press and public were still looking at works of art through a prism of sedate and proper bourgeois morality.

MAX SCHMITT

IN A SINGLE SCULL

Oil on canvas, by Thomas Eakins, 1871

The Alfred N. Punnett Purchase, 1934, Fund and

Gift of George D. Pratt, (34.92)

Compared with the impressionist canvases on the adjacent walls, Eakins's picture of rowers on the Schuylkill is as lucid as a snapshot. "Photographic realism," you might say, but in fact the phrase is a misnomer. I do not doubt that Eakins took photographs as preparatory studies—but only for the details. When he finally laid down his pencil and compass and picked up his brushes, every shape, size, and reflection had been preassembled like the mechanism of a watch. Monet was fond of painting symmetries of water and sky. Here Eakins has bested the Frenchman, because he achieved the same equilibrium without resorting to the blurriness of an inkblot. It is miraculous, in fact, how overtly Eakins has doubled every motif without our noticing it. Even Schmitt's scull has, besides its natural reflection, a "reflection" in the sky—the thin streak of cloud. This kind of ingeniousness would leave me cold if it were the sum and total of the picture. But it isn't, of course. Eakins orchestrated all these devices of visual harmony to augment his larger purpose: to capture a spiritual moment in everyday life, in this case, the harmony of two friends sharing the matchless beauty of fresh air, cool water, and infinite sky.

ARQUES-LA-BATAILLE

Oil on canvas, by John H. Twachtman, 1885

Morris K. Jesup Fund Purchase, 1968 (68.52)

This is a zen landscape painted by a Connecticut Yankee. The muted harmonies of one or two tonalities at most make this a counterpart to an étude by Claude Debussy. Twachtman is little known to the public, but he was by far the boldest and the most individual of the American Impressionists. Actually, his works are closer in spirit to Gauguin's than to Monet's. For this landscape of Normandy near Dieppe, Twachtman drew inspiration from two conflicting currents: the hypernaturalism of the French Impressionists and the near abstraction of Whistler. The result is one of the most completely accomplished nature studies by any artist in that crucial decade of emergent modernism, the 1880s.

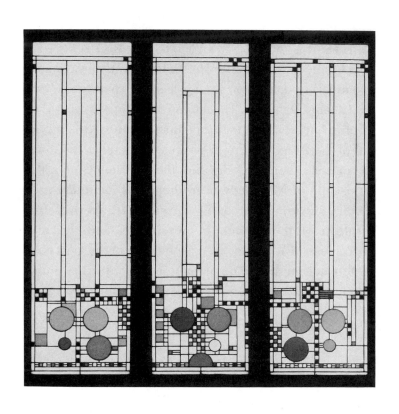

WINDOWS FROM THE
AVERY COONLEY
PLAYHOUSE

Stained-glass leaded windows by Frank Lloyd Wright, 1912

Purchase, 1967, Edward C. Moore, Jr., Gift and

Edgar J. Kaufmann Charitable Foundation Gift (67.231.1–3)

Genius in architectural design always lies in the details. Nowadays you find it in a building by Herman Kahn, who deliberately allowed wooden forms to impress their grain onto his poured concrete. Frank Lloyd Wright also paid close attention to detail, and his genius can be seen in the furniture and even in the windows of his houses and buildings. He learned this approach from Louis Sullivan, whose staircase from the Chicago Stock Exchange is installed in the Met opposite these windows. Wright is not known to have been a partisan of modern painting (he made the Guggenheim Museum into a wonderful building that is singularly inappropriate for the display of such), but these windows look as if he had worked from designs provided by Mondrian. In truth, the two men had very different sensibilities. Wright's design only toys with being reductive—he loved to pile up motifs to show off his energy and ingeniousness. But he could be whimsical too: notice his proud footnote of a tiny American flag inserted in the window at the far left.

MANTELPIECE FROM THE
VANDERBILT HOUSE

Marble, by Augustus Saint-Gaudens, with mosaic designed

by John La Farge, 1881–1882

Gift of Mrs. Cornelius Vanderbilt, Sr., 1925 (25.234)

First of all, remember that the
scale of this fireplace is wholly lost in its present setting.
It seems tucked away next to the courtyard like a monu-
ment in the side aisle of an Italian church. Of course, this
isn't an unflattering association, but Saint-Gaudens was
trying to convince you that the Vanderbilts had somehow
got their hands on a piece of the Parthenon. He has me
convinced. Can you imagine the impressiveness of this
marble statuary in a private residence? Here's the scene:
you have just been ushered into the entrance hall of the
Vanderbilts' cottage at Fifth Avenue and Fifty-seventh
Street. The butler withdraws, closing the door, and leaves
you standing face to face with a brace of life-size Greek
caryatids. You have to figure that nothing has left Athens
since the Elgin marbles, but who are you to underesti-
mate the Vanderbilts? This fireplace could as easily be
seen as clunky ostentation: in fact the mosaic by La Farge
is tepid classicism by the rules. I call your attention to
this structure solely on account of the statues by Saint-
Gaudens, one of the best American sculptors of any age.
He trod the accepted path of academicism, but he was
one of the few who breathed life into the old traditions
through his energetic carving and the outspoken, uncon-
ventional expressions of his figures.

HILT OF

A SMALL SWORD

Steel, with Wedgwood, English, late 18th c.

Gift of Stephen V. Grancsay, 1942 (42.50.46)

THIS IS A FINE, GAUDY, ENCRUSTED
object that I can admire without much reflection (if any)
on the essential purpose of swords. I doubt too that its first
owner was contemplating mayhem on the day that he sent
off to Wedgwood for these decorative inserts. Arms and
armor remained ceremonial long after the landed gentry
stopped exposing themselves to man-to-man combat.
Gentlemen of rank still wear swords at state occasions in
England, and the sceptered isles do a thriving tourist
trade based on the dress-up pageantry of their military past. I never imagined that I would see a sword
decorated with Wedgwood; strangely enough, though, it
looks right smart. Such delicacy should appear incongru-
ous on an instrument of war, and you might therefore say
that form has completely displaced function here—only
remember that this particular sword was made for sarto-
rial, not martial, effect.

PARADE HELMET

Embossed and chiseled steel,

by Filippo Negroli, Italian (Milan), 1543

Gift of J. Pierpont Morgan, 1917 (17.190.1720)

CLOTHES MAKE THE MAN, AND IF YOU were a sixteenth-century prince serious about your armor, you probably had your suit made in Milan. German armor has rightly enjoyed a distinguished reputation for getting the job done (preserving life and limb, literally), but the Italians were always the pacesetters of design. This extraordinary helmet looks to me like a sculpture that has the added advantage of being transportable on the head (for short periods only). The scholarly literature raises the possibility that this work was commissioned by Francis I, king of France. The High Mannerist style of its motifs would bear this out—Francis was an ardent admirer of Italian art. The grotesques, as these *rinceaux* and other hybrid ornaments are called, were the height of modern style in mid-sixteenth-century Rome. They were copied from the ancient Roman wall paintings that were being rediscovered (in grottoes—hence "grotesque") on a daily basis, almost, during the Renaissance, as Rome began to evolve from a medieval city into its present, timeless character. The crest of the helmet is a delectable mermaid, who appears supine in an attitude of surrender. She means business, though; she grasps (and studiously avoids the gaze of) the head of Medusa, which Perseus used to turn his adversaries into stone.

THE EMPEROR CALIGULA

Marble, Roman, 1st c.

Rogers Fund, 1914 (14.37)

Gaius caesar was a military brat, and the Roman soldiers gave him the nickname Caligula ("little boots") at the age of three. The combination of the childish and the brutal in this epithet was to be cruelly prophetic. Caligula has come to personify cruelty and despotism in public life, while his private history is shaded by reports of murder and incest. If this haughty and vain portrait head were unidentified, might we not still recognize that the subject was depraved? The head is raised imperiously: or is it inhumanly arrogant? Does the curve of the upper lip bespeak firmness that is wonted in a leader, or malevolence? The sculptor's ability to tread a fine line between expected flattery and the bitter truth may have saved him from becoming another morsel for the arena. Or maybe not.

URN IN THE FORM
OF A CYLINDRICAL BASKET

Marble, Roman, Imperial period (1st–2nd c.)

Gift of Mrs. Frederick E. Guest, 1937 (37.129 a-b)

Y OU HAVE TO LOOK HARD TO FIND
this marble basket at knee level concealed behind an
impressive array of portrait busts. At least there's no danger of confusing this piece with anything else in this gallery. Just look around: the Romans took an attitude of
high seriousness toward art: they preferred to make
statues of gods, emperors, or even solid citizens. No fun-
loving Hellenism for them: the engineers and empire
builders couldn't be that playful in public. (At home was
a different story, of course.) There is something incongru-
ous—even touching—about a quotidian and discardable
basket of flexible fiber reproduced in unyielding, imper-
ishable marble. This piece was probably carved as an urn
for ashes or for some other ritual use, so the sculptor was
only following orders. He diligently traced the curving
weave of the basket with mathematical exactness. A Hellenistic Greek would have delighted in all the cracks and
accidents of the original, but this anonymous Roman has
characteristically reduced the basket to its essential
geometry, as if he had an inclination toward Cubism.

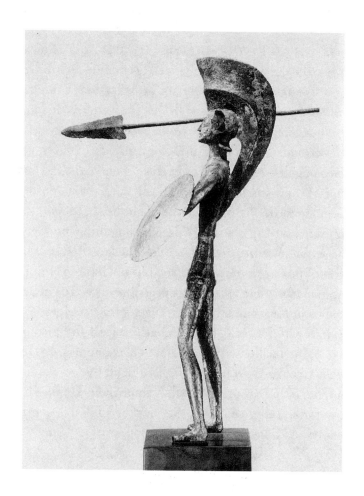

STATUETTE

OF A WARRIOR

Bronze, Etruscan (Italy), 5th c. B.C.

Bequest of Walter C. Baker, 1971 (1972.118.53)

216

TOUR IV

91

ALTHOUGH SLIGHT IN STATURE, this wiry little bronze bristles with menace. None of his companions in this glass case are anything like so rude—or vital. I prefer my warrior friend, who indicates in no uncertain terms his eagerness to stick me with his spear. His helmet is too big for him, and if he were any less threatening he might seem slightly comical. But there's no question about his seriousness. This statuette dates from the fifth century B.C., a critical period for the Etruscans: during this century the Romans began to flex their muscles, and suddenly everyone else on the Italian Peninsula felt crowded. Tall and graceful, this Etruscan warrior gives nonetheless an emphatic impression of strength. Now try his profile: he disappears! I wonder whether Alberto Giacometti knew Etruscan bronzes—he's the only other sculptor who could instill life into sticks of metal.

STATUETTE OF AN ATHLETE, THE "DIADOUMENOS"

Terra-cotta, Greek (Asia Minor), about 100 B.C.

Fletcher Fund, 1932 (32.11.2)

Most people regard classical art as the exclusive preserve of specialists, which is too bad. True, what we find are mostly Roman copies of lost Greek originals, and copies of course vary widely in merit. The Greek and Roman galleries of every major museum including the Metropolitan hold their share of sculptures that are long on age but plenty scarce on artistic interest. So we have to keep our eyes open: I keep coming back to these galleries in the hope of finding a jewel nestled amid a lot of cold stone. For instance, could any statuette by Clodion (French, eighteenth century) be fresher or more sensuous than this terra-cotta of the Diadoumenos, the youth who ties a fillet around his head? A discovery like this does not come from reading the labels. This one says the same thing all the others do: "copy after a lost work"—in this case, a life-size bronze by Polyclitus, the greatest sculptor from the period of the purest Greek classicism (440 B.C.). You simply have to look at all these things for yourself. Just compare the vivacity of this terra-cotta to the big but unexciting marble next to it. Looking at the musculature of the little Diadoumenos, you suddenly realize that you are admiring the genius of an untraceable artist, who at some unknowable time used his hands to transform a lump of clay into a graceful, poignant paean to ideal human beauty.

STATUETTE OF A
VEILED DANCER

Bronze, Greek, 2nd c. B.C.

Bequest of Walter C. Baker, 1971 (1972.118.95)

A DANCER WRAPPED FROM HEAD TO TOE: her body hidden and her movements constrained. Yet the dancer acts in concert with her drapery to form gestures and silhouettes that reveal the figure underneath and draw fleeting patterns of folds across the surface. The same words could describe the great American dancer Martha Graham. The difference is that Graham's choreography is devoted to the evocation of visual and even emotional abstractions. This dancer from Hellenistic Greece is much too overtly voluptuous to win a place in the Graham repertory. She is unabashedly erotic, however much she is confined. The charged rays of her drapery pull our eyes around her lithe figure, bidding us to move in counterpoint, a partner in her dance. She offers conflicting gestures of acceptance and refusal all at once. The artful concealment of mouth and breasts, the revealing thrust of elbow and leg, culminate in the tension between the violent turning away of her head and the alluring, palm-outward invitation of her hand.

MARIONETTE

Wood, cloth, and metal, Mali; Bamana people, 19th–20th c.

The Michael C. Rockefeller Memorial Collection,

Bequest of Nelson A. Rockefeller, 1979 (1979.206.52)

But is it art? this is the question that everyone asked when the Michael C. Rockefeller Wing opened in 1982. Doesn't the Museum of Natural History have all these things plus *dioramas*? I say, Congratulations! to the Metropolitan for rescuing the arts of Africa, the Pacific Islands, and the Americas from the shadow of fossils and minerals. Not every piece here is exciting, admittedly—for that matter, I am not enthralled by every Impressionist landscape that I see, and the Met has a truckload of those on view upstairs. This is a marionette made by an African culture that I cannot claim to know about. Are puppets art? I hope so, because this fragile concatenation of sticks and striped cloth is for me one of the most provocative works of art in this huge building. It looks strange to me in a way that is almost comical: my goodness, aren't these the prunelike features of Edith Sitwell, the quintessential English Plantagenet? But this figurine is not a joke, I have no doubt about that. A deeply serious artist has created a simulacrum of a human being, a sculpture that has an inner life, even if I can see through its cracks and joints. Although it is motionless now, I can imagine the magic that this marionette possessed when it was made to strut and fret emotions that are common to all existence.

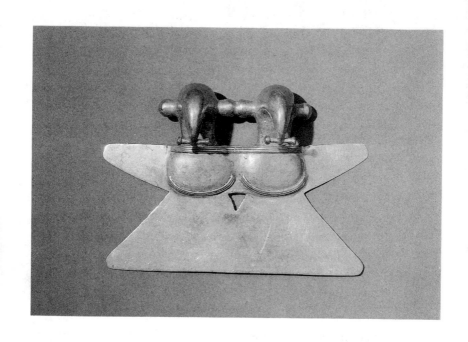

DOUBLE-HEADED
EAGLE PENDANT

Gold, Pre-Columbian, Costa Rican,

The Michael C. Rockefeller Memorial Collection,

Bequest of Nelson A. Rockefeller, 1979 (1979.206.538)

GOLDEN PENDANTS REPRESENTING eagles are among the most characteristic of ancient American art forms. The doubled motif of this one makes it exceptional, as does its high stylization: the result verges provocatively on abstraction. A child might say that this is a pair of paper dolls cut from a sheet of gold. I see here the silhouette of the wings against the sky—or perhaps their shadow skimming along the ground. However simple this pendant may appear, only centuries of seeing nature and comprehending it could have inspired the marvelous curve that distills the essence of an eagle into the shape of its predatory beak.

HORN BLOWER

Bronze, African (Nigeria), Court of Benin, 16th–17th c.

The Michael C. Rockefeller Memorial Collection,

Gift of Nelson A. Rockefeller, 1972 (1978.412.310)

LONG BEFORE EUROPEANS SET FOOT
in tropical Africa, Benin was a powerful nation with
sophisticated art. For five centuries a law-abiding people
were ruled there by their king. The Benin had no written
language; instead they left an eloquent record of their civilization in the bronze and ivory sculptures with which the
king adorned his palace, his court, and his own person.
The subject of this bronze was a musician who accompanied the religious dances at court. He took his job very
seriously. His head is capped with a helmet, and he grips
his horn with pride, the way a soldier holds his gun. The
feet are thick and broad, and they look to me like the roots
of a great tropical tree. From these roots there surges a
powerful, supple, resilient trunk.

STATUETTE
OF A WOMAN

Marble, Cycladic, 3rd Millenium B.C.

Fletcher Fund, 1934 (34.11.3)

STANDING IN THE MIDST OF SIMILAR works, only this statuette of a woman possesses an aura of sensuality and inaccessibility. The extreme simplicity of form does not disturb our twentieth-century eyes—on the contrary, we read it as extreme sophistication. The remote culture of the Cyclades in the Aegean produced such sculptures in prolific numbers, but most of them have barely more life than the stones from which they were carved. This statuette is an astonishing exception. The outline of her figure traces an invisible boundary between geometric abstraction and feminine grace. Cycladic sculptors typically suppressed such features as the eyes, hair, and belly in order to heighten the allure of other feminine attributes. The immense gulf that separates this figurine from our time and culture, the obscurity of the sculptor's motives in creating her, only enhance her mysterious appeal. She is exquisitely reticent.

GERTRUDE STEIN

Oil on canvas, by Pablo Picasso, 1906

Bequest of Gertrude Stein, 1946 (47.106)

THIS IS THE ONE TIME THAT THE irrepressible Picasso met his match: he really felt threatened by the assignment to paint Gertrude Stein, the brooding, lumpish, and heaven-knows-what-else guru of prewar Paris. According to Alice B. Toklas, Picasso required ninety sittings from Stein, and finally he obliterated the face in desperation. Later, back in his studio, he painted in a face based on an African mask. (This all took place during the time of his *Demoiselles d'Avignon*, now in the Museum of Modern Art.) This great head, portrayed as if made of stone, is enough to make an unforgettable picture. Picasso wanted to paint a twentieth-century oracle, and he succeeded. Still, every other part of the painting bears witness to his struggle: the background is fudged, purely and simply. He couldn't decide what to do. Was it really Picasso who labored over the white ruffles of Stein's blouse, or some tenth-rate academic hack? Ultimately, though, none of this matters—we always return to that awesome head.

I SAW THE FIGURE 5 IN GOLD

Oil on composition board, by Charles Demuth, 1928

Alfred Stieglitz Collection, 1949 (49.59.1)

WITH THIS PAINTING DEMUTH INVENTED
Pop Art thirty years early—except that *I Saw the Figure 5
in Gold* was painted as a homage to a poem written by a
friend, not as social satire. The poet William Carlos Williams had described in words the clamor of a fire engine
screaming through city streets. It is a good poem, but I
think Demuth's painting is better. I like that Demuth
appropriated for his title the only two lines in Williams
that scan like verse. With or without the reference to fire
trucks, we have to step aside in the face of these uncoiling
5s. Although Picasso and the other Cubists had already
discovered the value of letters and words as elements of
design, Demuth was the first painter to exploit the expressive power of the naked symbol wrenched out of context.
The Pop artists Jasper Johns (American flag) and Robert
Indiana (LOVE) liked this idea well enough to base their
careers on it. On the other hand, kids love this painting
strictly because of the fire engines, and there's nothing
wrong with that. Demuth provided some word games for
the young at heart. See if you can find three references to
his friend's name.

HISTORY OF NAVIGATION, FROM THE OCEAN LINER NORMANDIE

Reverse-painted glass, French, 1934

Gift of Dr. and Mrs. Irwin R. Berman, 1976 (1976.414.3)

CONGRATULATIONS ON COMPLETING the course. You deserve some refreshment: kindly repair to the cappuccino bar in the Museum Restaurant and pull up a chair to one of the café tables. Your backdrop is a reminder, a happy survivor, of the luxury of a bygone age: France between the wars. Let yourself drift into the sleek escapism of Art Deco. This mural was one of four such painted glass adornments to the grand salon of the ocean liner *Normandie*. Can you imagine the reflections of a dozen chandeliers? (Now add the gowns by Balenciaga and Worth.) You are looking at a glorious amalgam of irreconcilable tastes: Beaux Arts academicism, a hopeless infatuation with technology, and the montage editings of the avant-garde cinema (pioneered by Eisenstein in a movie named after another ship, *Potemkin*—but, never fear, this piece couldn't be further from Socialist Realism). Selective, eclectic, idiosyncratic, this glass wall bears as much relation to the history of navigation as the guide you hold bears to the standard histories of art. But as compensation for its disregard for chronology and comprehensiveness, this souvenir of the *Normandie* offers an indubitable stylishness and savoir faire. *A Connoisseur's Guide to the Met* is my attempt to strike the same kind of bargain. Now you're on your own. *Bon voyage.*

Paul Magriel's legendary career as a connoisseur and independent curator has spanned five decades. He is widely recognized for his pioneering scholarship in the history of boxing and the history of dance. As a collector, he was an early and influential appreciator of such diverse fields as American still-life painting, American figure drawings, and art nouveau glass. His collection of Renaissance bronzes was acquired intact by a major American museum. Exhibitions selected by Paul Magriel have appeared in museums across the United States. He lives in New York City.

John T. Spike is a noted historian of Italian art. Since earning his Doctor of Philosophy degree at Harvard University in 1979, Dr. Spike has served as guest curator to many major museums, including the National Gallery of Art and the Kimbell Art Museum in Fort Worth. He has published numerous articles and books on aspects of European painting and sculpture. John Spike lives in New York City with his wife, Michelle, and their son Nicholas.